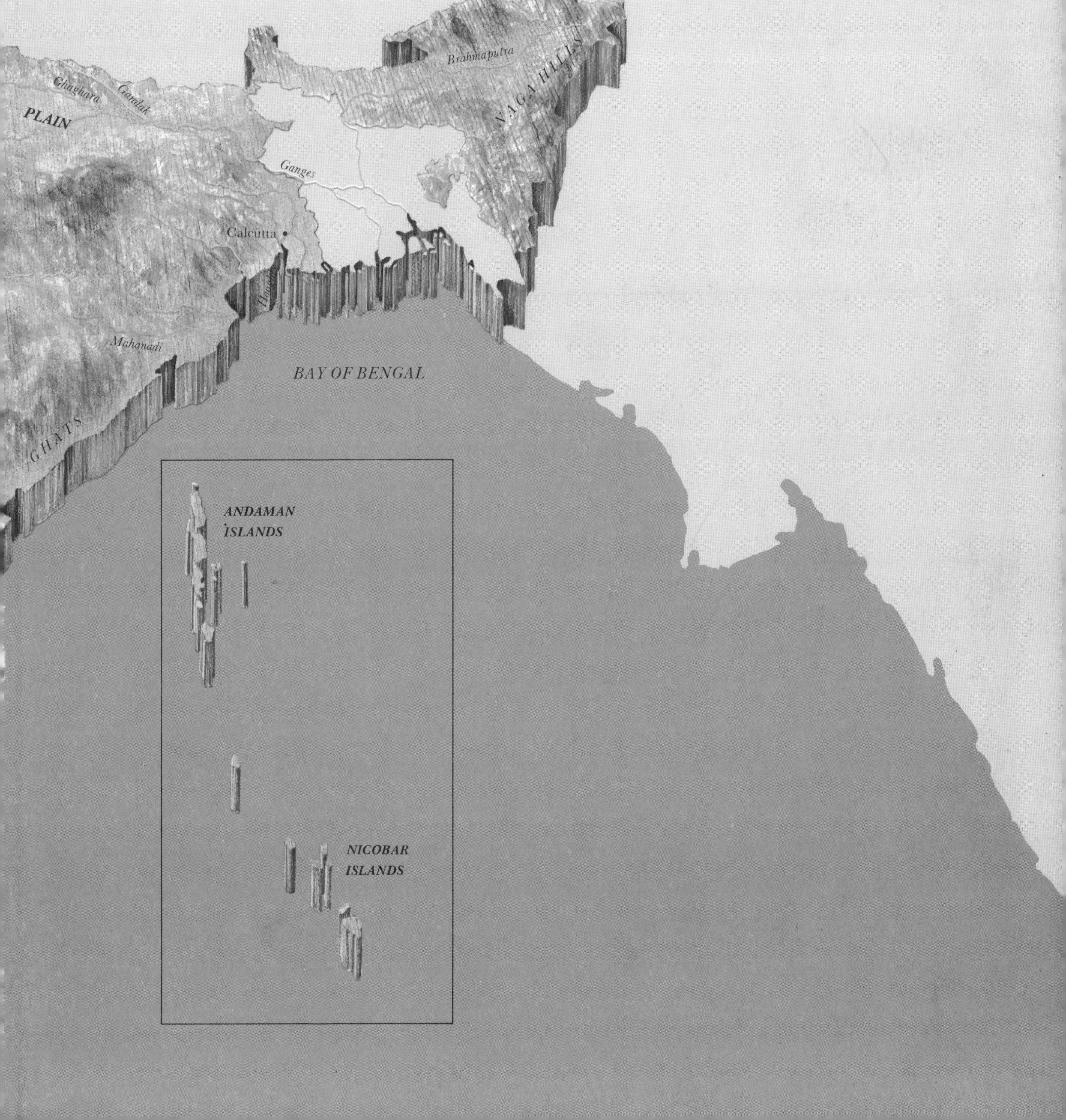
Ghaghara
Gandak
PLAIN
Brahmaputra
NAGA HILLS
Ganges
Calcutta
Hooghly
Mahanadi
BAY OF BENGAL
GHATS
ANDAMAN ISLANDS
NICOBAR ISLANDS

INDIA

सत्यमेव जयते

INDIA

By the Editors of Time-Life Books

TIME-LIFE BOOKS ◦ ALEXANDRIA, VIRGINIA

Other Publications:

FIX IT YOURSELF
FITNESS, HEALTH & NUTRITION
SUCCESSFUL PARENTING
HEALTHY HOME COOKING
UNDERSTANDING COMPUTERS
THE ENCHANTED WORLD
THE KODAK LIBRARY OF
CREATIVE PHOTOGRAPHY
GREAT MEALS IN MINUTES
THE CIVIL WAR
PLANET EARTH
COLLECTOR'S LIBRARY OF THE CIVIL WAR
THE EPIC OF FLIGHT
THE GOOD COOK
WORLD WAR II
HOME REPAIR AND IMPROVEMENT
THE OLD WEST

This volume is one in a series of books describing countries of the world — their natural resources, peoples, histories, economies and governments.

For information on and a full description of any of the Time-Life Books series listed above, please write:
Reader Information
Time-Life Books
541 North Fairbanks Court
Chicago, Illinois 60611

Cover: Wicker lanterns hanging on tall bamboo poles glow beside the Ganges River at Varanasi. The lamps have been lighted for an autumn festival known as Akash Deep, when the spirits of the dead are said to make an annual visit to earth; the lights help them find their way back to their heavenly abode.

LIBRARY OF NATIONS

Series Editor: Ellen Galford

Editorial Staff for *India*
Editor: Gillian Moore
Researcher: Susie Dawson
Designer: Mary Staples
Sub-editor: Jane Hawker
Picture Department: Christine Hinze, Peggy Tout
Editorial Assistant: Molly Oates

EDITORIAL PRODUCTION
Production Assistants: Nikki Allen, Maureen Kelly
Editorial Department: Theresa John, Debra Lelliott

Valuable help was given in the preparation of this volume by Deepak Puri (New Delhi).

Contributors: The chapter texts were written by Sarah Hobson, Trevor Fishlock, Sumi Krishna, Alan Lothian and Gillian Tindall.

Assistant Editor for the U.S. Edition: Barbara Fairchild Quarmby

Pages 1 and 2: India's national emblem, shown on page 1, is a rendering of a sculpture erected by the Emperor Ashoka in the third century B.C. The emblem shows three lions mounted on an abacus decorated with a bull, a wheel and a galloping horse. Below it appear the words "truth alone triumphs." The wheel from Ashoka's column appears again on India's flag, which is shown on page 2. The wheel's many spokes link its center with its circumference, symbolizing unity in diversity.

CONSULTANTS

Dr. George Morrison Carstairs, formerly Professor of Psychiatry at Edinburgh University, is the author of *The Twice-Born,* a psychological study of Indian villagers.

Ian Jack is a journalist who has covered India for *The Sunday Times* since 1976.

Dr. H. A. Kanitkar is a lecturer in the extramural department of London University's School of Oriental and African Studies. She specializes in Hinduism and Hindu culture.

First printing.
Printed in U.S.A.
Published simultaneously in Canada.
School and library distribution by Silver Burdett Company, Morristown, New Jersey.

Library of Congress Cataloguing in Publication Data
India.
(Library of nations)
Bibliography: p.
Includes index.
1. India. I. Time-Life Books. II. Series:
Library of nations (Alexandria, Va.)
DS407.I444 1987 954 87-1979
ISBN 0-8094-5173-5 (lib. bdg.)
ISBN 0-8094-5172-7

Front and back endpapers: A topographic map showing the main rivers, plains, mountain ranges and other natural features of India appears on the front endpaper. The back endpaper shows the country's states and territories, as well as the major cities. Two disputed areas outside the jurisdiction of India are indicated by dotted lines on the back endpaper. Pakistan controls the disputed area to the northwest of the state of Jammu and Kashmir, China that to the east of the state; India, however, claims both zones.

CONTENTS

Sculpted into the hillsides of the Tumkur district in the southwestern state of Karnataka, steeply terraced rice paddies catch and hold every drop of rain

water. Sown over a quarter of India's cultivated land, rice is the nation's principal crop. Only China's harvest is larger.

In a family planning clinic in a West Bengal village, a doctor describes the workings of an intrauterine device to a young mother. During the 1970s,

THE EXPLODING POPULATION

India's population of more than 750 million is growing at a rate of more than one million a month. One sixth of all people alive today are Indian. Only the Chinese are more numerous, and the Indians are almost sure to overtake the Chinese by the mid-21st century if they continue to increase at the current rate.

The cause of the population surge is a sharply declining death rate, which has not yet been paralleled by a fall in births. Public health measures, such as smallpox inoculation and providing cleaner drinking water, have raised life expectancy from 32 years in the 1940s to 55 in the 1980s. Meanwhile, the average Indian couple has four or five children, and few use contraceptives. In the country, where even children help in the fields, large families are still thought desirable.

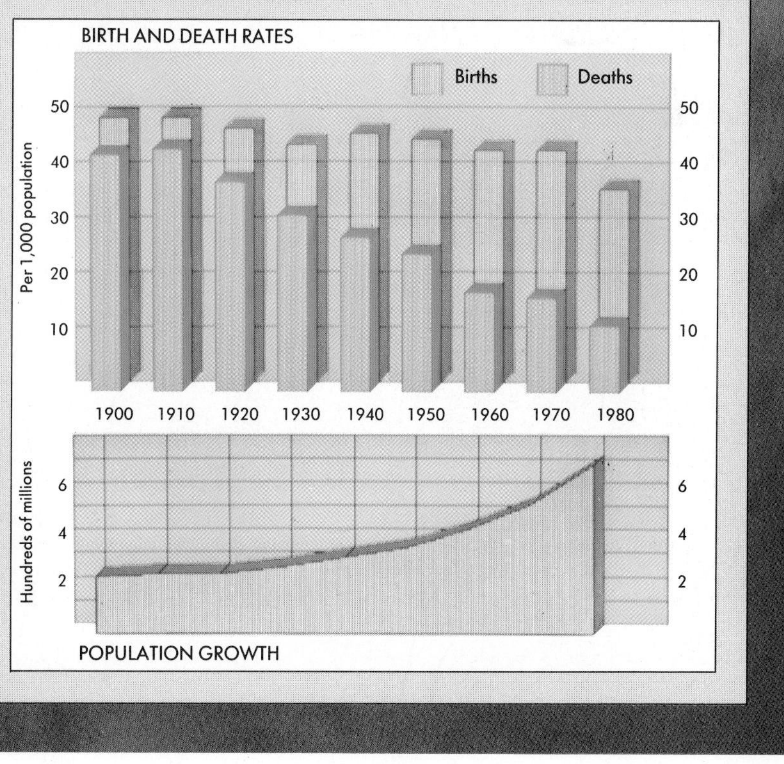

government birth-control campaigns concentrated primarily on sterilization, but now the emphasis has shifted toward IUDs, condoms and oral pills.

A GIANT FILM INDUSTRY

The Indian motion picture industry is the world's largest, employing about two million people in the production of more than 700 features a year. Every week, some 70 million Indians stand in line to see the latest releases. Until recently, the industry was highly profitable, and provided an important source of revenue for the state governments, which levy an average tax of 60 percent on box-office sales. In the early 1980s, however, television and videos began to make serious inroads into the profits of the film industry.

Despite the industry's size, the number of stars is small. Most movies draw on a handful of popular actors, who often work on 20 productions at once. Their scripts are virtually indistinguishable variations on the boy-meets-girl theme, punctuated with song and dance routines. There is also a tradition of social documentary, which until recently had minority appeal; however, in the 1980s, films with such themes as the role of women and political corruption have been box-office successes.

From hand-painted posters atop a cinema in Bangalore, Indian film stars gaze down at their public. The billboards advertise a movie in the local tongue of

Kannada, one of several southern languages in which films are made in Madras studios. Bombay, the Hollywood of India, makes movies mainly in Hindi.

A HERITAGE OF SACRED BUILDINGS

India's architectural inspiration achieved its fullest expression in sacred buildings. The landscape of the subcontinent is punctuated with temples built by Hindus, Buddhists and Jains, adherents of the country's three great indigenous faiths. Spanning 20 centuries, the places of worship take numerous forms, but one constant feature is intricate ornamentation, especially on the buildings' exteriors. Columns appear in every conceivable shape, from spiral to 16-sided, and all available surfaces are embellished with abstract motifs, or carvings of gods and goddesses, plants and mythical beasts.

In every town and village are found the shrines of all the religions practiced there. In addition, India boasts some spectacular temple complexes, miniature cities in themselves, which grew up over many lifetimes. A number of these collections of beautiful buildings were erected by the Jains, who make up only 0.5 percent of India's population but, because they believe that temple construction helps procure salvation, have contributed disproportionately to the country's architectural heritage.

The spires of Shatrunjaya, a Jain temple-city of 863 shrines, reach toward the heavens in the mountains of Gujarat. Most of the buildings date from the

17th century, but some earlier structures remain. Shatrunjaya is one of the most important places of pilgrimage for Jains.

A load of wheat chaff in a tall cane basket tips precariously as a farmer encourages his oxen along a narrow track in a village in Rajasthan. Although tractors are slowly becoming more common in the Indian countryside, oxcarts are still in daily use.

COMPLEXITIES OF A TEEMING LAND

India can steal the traveler's heart and brand his soul like no other country. For centuries, its landscape, its sounds and smells, its people have stimulated the imagination of Westerners, causing them often to marvel and sometimes to despair. "So far as I am able to judge," wrote Mark Twain, "nothing has been left undone, either by man or nature, to make India the most extraordinary country that the sun visits on his round. Nothing seems to have been forgotten, nothing overlooked."

Twain—the pen name of American writer and traveler Samuel Clemens—went to India in 1896. His job was to describe it. He nearly threw away his pen in defeat. "Always," he wrote, "when you think you have come to the end of her tremendous specialties and have finished hanging tags upon her as . . . the Land of the Plague, the Land of Famine, the Land of Giant Illusions, the Land of Stupendous Mountains and so forth, another specialty crops up and another tag is required." It was best, he decided, to discard the labels and call it simply the Land of Wonders.

Those wonders have been described by writers ever since the Greeks, the first ambassadors of Western civilization, reached India in the third century B.C. The travelers have left us with an impression of the country that is a series of isolated scenes, all true but only fractions of a greater truth: the Taj Mahal at midnight and poverty at noon, the dust of the listless plains, the color and clamor of the bazaars, elephants moving gently through lush forests. Running through nearly all the images are sun and water—unyielding heat, great rivers—potent symbols of the sources of life throughout the world, but nowhere more obviously so than in India.

India has experienced hundreds of years of foreign invasion and influence, yet it still manages somehow to absorb and change everything the world cares to impose on it, remaining at its core untouched. India, in a word, is "different," which is why the rest of the world chooses to see it as mysterious.

Although it is modernizing rapidly, India still moves according to ancient cultural rhythms and hallowed social practices. The seventh-largest country in the world, with a population of more than 730 million, it has an economy among the world's top 15; yet 70 percent of its people live off the land as their ancestors did and struggle to subsist. It has millions who enjoy educational standards approaching those of the West, while more than 60 percent of the population cannot read. It has research foundations both for space vehicles and for oxcarts. Its young executives and civil servants have marriages arranged for them by their parents, who believe that the institution has far too important a role in cementing society to be undermined by such uncertainties as youthful love.

The stabilizing power of tradition is

1

evident everywhere in India, a country that rejects almost nothing of its heritage. Its history begins as far back as 2500 B.C., when a great urban civilization sprang up in the valley of the Indus—the river that runs through present-day Pakistan but gave India its name. Indus Valley culture flourished for 1,000 years—until the invasions of Aryan peoples from central Asia. These nomadic tribes brought their own gods and social customs to India, but as they settled across the land, they absorbed many of the traditions and religious beliefs of the indigenous peoples—including those of the Indus Valley civilization.

One outcome of this blending of cultures was the immensely complex Hindu religion, with its hundreds of gods and its doctrine of the transmigration of souls from one earthly existence to another. The fusion of cultures also gave rise to the caste system that structures Hindu society to this day, assigning each individual to a closed group with its own obligations and taboos. India has thousands of different castes. The members of each caste order their lives so as to minimize contact with outsiders, believing that they will be contaminated by the food, water or touch of those lower in the hierarchy.

After the Aryan influx, other waves of invaders periodically encroached on India from the north. Most notable among them were the Moguls, adherents to the Islamic faith, who created an Indian empire that lasted from the 16th to the 19th century. Then came an epoch of European dominance. The Portuguese reached Indian shores in the 15th century, the Dutch in the 16th century and the French in the 17th century—but it was the British, who first arrived as traders in 1608, who succeeded to the Indian empire of the Moguls. In the mid-18th century, the British became effective rulers of Bengal and steadily expanded their sphere of influence. By the mid-19th century, they were masters of all India. They governed until the subcontinent gained its independence in 1947. Provinces to the northwest and northeast then seceded on religious grounds, and took their freedom as Islamic Pakistan; another secession in 1971 transformed East Pakistan into Bangladesh.

Most of the territorial subcontinent retained the title of India. It chose a democratic form of government and today is the largest democracy in the world. It became a republic, but it remained within the Commonwealth.

India is still strewn with reminders of this long and complicated history. Its most famous monument, the Taj Mahal at Agra, was built by a 17th-century Muslim emperor as a memorial to his dead wife. In the main city of the small territory of Goa, a Portuguese colony until 1961, there stands a statue to a local overlord of old, bearing the Portuguese inscription: "D.M.C. Dias—a great man, recognized by his homeland." In Calcutta's Great Eastern Hotel, frequented in the past by the author Rudyard Kipling, a window in the lobby bears to this day the gilt-lettered inscription: "By appointment to H.M. the King Emperor and H.M. the Queen Empress." Other former colonies would have done away with their imperial relics, but such gestures are alien to India.

Another testimony to Indians' capacity to absorb, rather than dismantle, is the large number of religions practiced on the subcontinent. Hinduism easily predominates, claiming 82 percent of the population, but the Indian Constitution makes it clear that no religion in the republic has precedence over any other as far as the state is concerned.

In India, there are more than 75 million Muslims—ironically, about as many as there are in Pakistan. The next largest minority is Christian, with 18 million followers. A substantial Christian community has thrived in southwestern India since the first century A.D.; many of the Christians elsewhere on the subcontinent descend from mixed marriages contracted between Hindu women and British men in the 18th and 19th centuries. There are 14 million Sikhs, whose religion, launched in the 15th century, is a blend of Hindu polytheism and Islamic monotheism. Originally, the creed was pacifist, but at the end of the 18th century, the Sikhs became militant in response to Muslim persecution. Proud of their martial tradition, the Sikhs in time of need have proved reckless warriors. In modern times, the Sikhs have earned a reputation for being hard-working businessmen, farmers, doctors, engineers and taxi drivers. Relations between Sikhs and Hindus have often been close, and mixed marriages are frequent.

Buddhism has five million followers in India, where it originated in the sixth century B.C. Like Hinduism, it teaches that souls progress from one earthly vehicle to another, but it rejects the Hindu division of society into castes. There are also 3.5 million Jains, members of a sect that began during the same period as Buddhism and resembles it in many ways. Neither faith posits a creator or first cause for the universe; both teach reverence for all living things, no matter how lowly. The Jains number among them the most ascetic holy men and some of the wealthiest businessmen to be found on the

Reflected by the sacred pool, the gilded walls of the Golden Temple at Amritsar shimmer in the early-morning light. The temple, the Sikhs' holiest shrine, is in the northwestern state of Punjab — the religion's heartland, where 80 percent of India's Sikhs live.

entire subcontinent today. There are about 100,000 Parsis—followers of Zoroaster—whose religion moved eastward from Persia after its foundation in the fifth century B.C. There are a few hundred Jews, mostly in the big cities and the southwest.

An important minority of India's population follow none of these religions. India's tribal peoples, many of them descendants of the subcontinent's aboriginal populations, have their own religions, and most of them are animists, who venerate the mysterious forces embodied in wood or water or animal life. There are more than 400 Scheduled Tribes—so called because their names are listed in the Constitution, which specifies that they must be protected from social injustice and all forms of exploitation. The members of these tribes number some 50 million. They are widely distributed throughout the subcontinent. In the past, most of them lived in forests, where they were relatively isolated from the outside world. As India's population expanded and the forests shrank, however, many of the tribal peoples came into regular contact with Hindu villagers. In spite of growing proximity to a more sophisticated civilization, few tribal people have intermarried with other Indians, and some of them have held fast to the customs that distinguish them from their neighbors.

The Chenchus are an example of a tribe that has maintained an almost stone-age existence. These people, who inhabit the mountains on either side of the Krishna river in southern India, are forest nomads who, until a generation ago, subsisted by gathering fruits and nuts and hunting game with a bow and arrow. Today, most of the 18,000 Chenchus have abandoned this traditional lifestyle, but a minority have persisted in it. They still wear little clothing, alternate their dwelling places between a bamboo hut and an overhanging rock, and offer the first fruits of the season to a god they call Garelamaisama, the deity of the forest and hunt. They have, however, entered the cash economy: They sell honey and forest products with pharmaceutical uses to a cooperative in a nearby town, and they buy grain with the proceeds.

Some tribal groups long ago progressed from hunting and gathering to slash-and-burn cultivation, and others are settled agriculturists. The Apa Tanis, from a mountain valley near India's northeastern border, cultivate rice and other crops on irrigated terraces and produce extremely high yields despite never having come to terms with the plow. They maintain contact with a spirit world through shamans, marry strictly within their own group and speak a tongue that is totally different from Assamese, the language spoken by nearby Hindus.

Languages are another commodity that India has in profusion: The most obvious reason is the sheer size of the country. But limited horizons have also been a crucial factor. The majority of Indians have always been peasants subsisting off the soil; communications were almost nonexistent until the last century, except along major rivers, and people rarely traveled more than a week's walk from their villages. Even today, although India contains some vast cities including four with more than four million inhabitants, three quarters of the people live in the countryside. The small village where a few hundred people dwell is much more typical of this subcontinent than the metropolis. In India's thousands of virtually self-contained communities,

The predominant racial type in India is Caucasian but some minorities, especially in the Himalayas, have Mongolian features. This sample of regional portraits includes, from left to right: a woman from Pune, near the west coast, draped in the sari worn throughout India; a young man from Kashmir, with the blue eyes often seen in this northern state; a girl from the east coast, her braids looped up in a style favored for children; a man from Rajasthan, whose bright turban is characteristic of that state; and a Mongolian woman from the Ladakh region, near the Tibetan border.

speech acquired local idiosyncracies that it has never lost.

At the broadest level of categorization, the Indian government recognizes 15 major languages, each at least as different from the next as English, French and German. One of them is Sanskrit, the classical language of India, spoken widely by the Aryans until the 10th century but now reserved for religious and scholarly uses. Sanskrit and the languages of Europe share the same ancient roots. Eleven of the major languages spoken today in India originated from Sanskrit; one, Urdu, is a fusion of a Sanskrit-derived language and Persian. The remaining four major tongues, Tamil being the oldest, belong to the Dravidian language family, which may be indigenous to India. To compound communication problems, most of the 15 languages are written in distinctly different scripts.

When India promulgated its Constitution in 1950, Hindi—one of the derivatives of Sanskrit—was decreed to be the nation's official language. It has remained so ever since, and India's own name for itself, Bharat, is a Hindi word. The decision in favor of Hindi held considerable political difficulties, because it is the native language of Hindus living in part of northern India. Southerners, in particular, who speak Tamil or one of the related languages, have fiercely resented what they see as a northern imposition. The language question has caused periodic agitation in provincial areas.

English, despite its associations with former imperialism, survives as the main language of government because it is the one tongue that every educated Indian knows. When politicians debate in the national Parliament, they do so in English. When the Communist party of India holds national conferences and inveighs against imperialism past and present, it does so in the speech that British viceroys used.

The 15 major languages are merely the beginning of the country's linguistic labyrinth. There are 97 recognizably different forms of Hindi alone, and a similar number of variations on the other languages. Scholars argue endlessly over whether one or another speech pattern should be regarded as a minor language or simply as a dialect within a major language. There is rarely any doubt over the idiosyncratic tongues of the tribal peoples. Otherwise, speech varies slightly from one village to the next, and all that can be confidently asserted is that there are several hundred different mother tongues in India, many incomprehensible to all the others.

Independent India was founded as a federal union, with a central all-Indian government and Parliament in the capital at Delhi, and regional governments and assemblies in each of 17 provincial states. Many of the state boundaries were inherited from the time of British rule and had been determined by historical accident rather than cultural logic. Since the departure of the British, boundaries have several times been redrawn to take cultural affiliations into account and, above all, to meet demands for linguistic unity. Today, there are 23 semiautonomous states and, in addition, a clutch of small territories administered by the union government in Delhi. The union territories include Goa and Pondicherry—former colonies of Portugal and France respectively, which remained separate from the new India for some years after Independence—and Delhi itself.

Each of the states and territories has

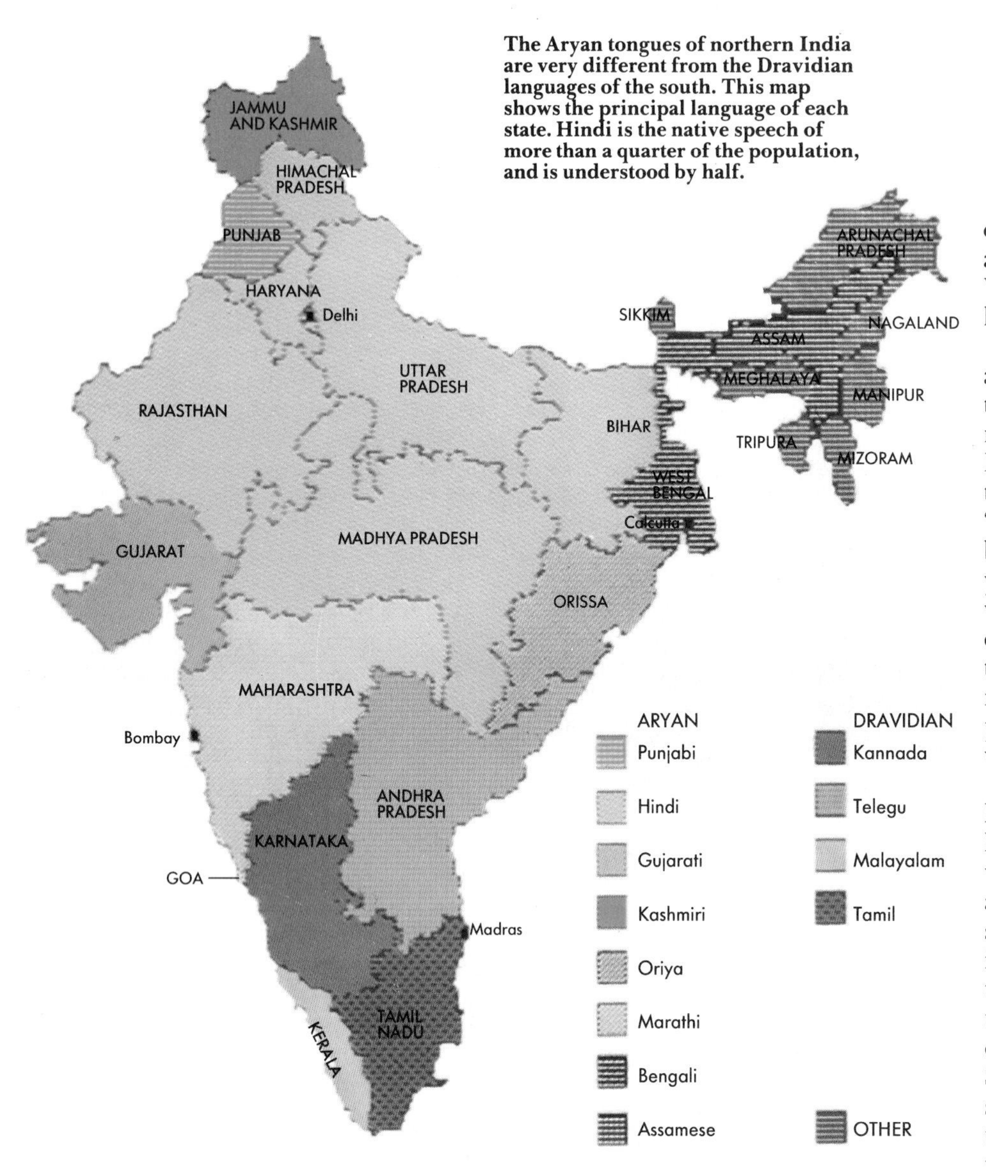

The Aryan tongues of northern India are very different from the Dravidian languages of the south. This map shows the principal language of each state. Hindi is the native speech of more than a quarter of the population, and is understood by half.

a character very much its own. From one to the next, the landscape can change from arid savanna to tropical rain forest, from featureless plain to soaring mountains. The people, their history and their traditions vary just as dramatically. Consequently, between the Himalayas and Cape Comorin, it is virtually impossible to generalize. Practically every rule of Indian life has at least one glaring exception.

India's capital, Delhi, lies in the north of the country in the vast, sun-baked plain of the greatest river in the land, the Ganges. In this city is preserved a vast sweep of India's history. From the 12th century onward, successive Hindu and Muslim dynasties focused their empires on this spot, and monuments from the past abound in the suburbs and in Old Delhi. Adjacent New Delhi is the seat of government today. The grandiose government buildings raised by the British were finished in 1931—just 16 years before they relinquished their rule. Independent India took over these testimonies to imperial glory and directed them to national ends: What was the viceroy's palace now houses the Indian president.

To the northwest of Delhi lies a vital area of the subcontinent, an area where the complex heritage from the past has not been absorbed as peaceably as in Delhi. Punjab—originally a larger area than the present state—literally means "land of the five rivers." It has always been abundantly watered by Himalayan torrents, and nowadays, irrigation via drilled wells and canals makes it an extremely fertile farmland. Over the two decades beginning in 1960, dramatic improvements in agricultural productivity brought considerable wealth to the region.

Historically, Punjab had a particularly rich variety of racial, religious and linguistic characteristics; as a result, the western partition line between India and Pakistan was drawn in 1947 straight down the middle of the province. The part allotted to Pakistan contained a majority of Muslims; the population of the eastern half was fairly evenly divided between Hindus and Sikhs. But many people found themselves on the wrong side of the linguistic and religious border, and for a few weeks in 1947, there was an outbreak of communal violence as both groups fought their way to relative safety.

For the next half-dozen years, the Indian Punjab shared a provincial capital—the old British hill station of Simla—with the neighboring mountain state of Himachal Pradesh (whose name means "the state of snow"). In 1953, Himachal Pradesh was allowed to have Simla all to itself, while Punjab acquired a brand-new capital city, Chandigarh, designed for the purpose by Swiss architect Le Corbusier. Even before the capital was completed, the Sikhs had begun to press for separate administrative arrangements. So in 1966, the Indian Punjab was partitioned: The majority of Hindus were contained in the new state of Haryana, and the Sikhs remained under the old territorial title.

But the division was not a clean one: The capital, Chandigarh, was shared by Haryana and truncated Punjab, which contained a slim majority of Sikhs. Some Sikhs had long dreamed of an independent nation of their own, which would be called Khalistan. By the 1980s, the agitation for independence reached violent levels. And in 1984, the unrest led to the storming of the Golden Temple at Amritsar by the Indian Army, which ended with many deaths on both sides. In retribution, Sikhs assassinated Prime Minister Indira Gandhi, in November of that year.

Immediately north of Punjab and Himachal Pradesh is the state of Jammu and Kashmir, composed of the plains of Jammu in the southwest and the Himalayan peaks and high villages of Kashmir. Like Punjab, Jammu and Kashmir has suffered because of its religious differences. Before Independence, it was part of the one third of India that was not controlled directly by the British: It was the foremost of the 562 princely states whose rulers, provided they fell in with British policy, continued to reign in the splendor they had enjoyed for centuries and even raised their own armies.

Jammu and Kashmir became a matter of dispute between India and Pakistan the moment Independence was declared, because of a historical accident. While 80 percent of the state's population in 1947 was Muslim, the ruler—Maharaja Hari Singh—was

Three porters haul a barrel of kerosene up a road in the hill town of Simla, once the summer capital of India. Founded by the British in the early 19th century as a refuge from the heat of the plains, Simla is now a popular resort for many middle-class Indians.

In the region of Ladakh, on the eastern edge of Jammu and Kashmir, a white-walled Buddhist monastery dominates a village on the steep slopes of a barren

landscape. This area, an extension of the 16,400-foot-high Tibetan plateau, is cut off from rain by the Himalayas to the south.

1

Hindu, as were most of the people inhabiting the Jammu part of his realm. Under the Independence arrangements, the rulers of princely states had the right to choose whether to throw their lot in with India or with Pakistan. Hari Singh was still agonizing over which course to take when a party of Pathan tribal warriors from Pakistan invaded the state. The Maharaja, in a panic, invited the Indians to help him. The two countries then engaged in a brisk war on Kashmiri territory before the United Nations stepped in and drew a cease-fire line down the middle of the old state. The area to the south and east was to be occupied by India, that to the north and west by Pakistan. The cease-fire line has remained an international boundary ever since. In 1949, the Maharaja abdicated his by-then-titular position in favor of his son.

In 1948, Jawaharlal Nehru, independent India's first prime minister, accepted in principle that there should be a referendum on sovereignty among the Kashmiris; but he and his successors failed to test public opinion in this way, and the dispute has still not been resolved. Occasionally, the region's Muslims have shown signs of unrest, even though they and the Hindu Kashmiris generally dwell amiably side by side. For Nehru and other Indian idealists, Jammu and Kashmir always had a more than strategic and territorial significance. Being a state where Muslims are in the majority, it stands as an affirmation of the avowedly secular nature of the Indian Constitution.

The state of Jammu and Kashmir is mostly an area of stupendous mountain scenery. Sheltered among the Himalayas is the beautiful vale of Kashmir, its fertile fruitgrowing slopes set off by jagged peaks. Many people spend the summer in houseboats on Dal Lake, in the center of the vale, retreating to dry land when winter causes the lake to freeze over. On the high eastern side of the state, near the border with Tibet, lies the region of Ladakh. Physically and ethnically, Ladakh resembles the land across the frontier, and it is one of the few remaining refuges of unsullied Tibetan Buddhism.

The great mountain bastion that divides India from central Asia stands as a backdrop to the states and union territories that project awkwardly to the northeast, all but cut off from the rest of India by the intervening shapes of Nepal and Bangladesh. Here, just seven million people are spread throughout seven different administrative areas. The reason for the proliferation of districts is that they contain the biggest concentration of tribes in the country; the boundaries closely follow racial and linguistic transitions.

These seven states and union territories, together with Assam—a state with its own substantial tribal population—are sometimes referred to as the North East Frontier. The land consists mostly of thickly forested hills, high enough to attract tremendous rainfall in the monsoon season. The zone around the village of Cherrapunji, in Meghalaya, is one of the wettest spots on earth, with an average annual rainfall of 426 inches, compared with 24 inches in London and 42 inches in New York. In June alone, at Cherrapunji, 98 inches of rain falls.

Besides sheltering the little-known tribes, those northeastern rain forests are also the home of a rich variety of wildlife, including the extremely rare one-horned Indian rhinoceros. There is virtually no industry, apart from the production of oil and tea in Assam. Tea

DANCING HEROIC TALES

Although many intricate forms of classical dance-drama have been traditional for millennia, one of the most popular in India today is the regional theater known as *kathakali*. This vigorous art form reached its current development between the 16th and 17th centuries in the southwestern state of Kerala. Drawing on the heroic myths and legends of Hindu religious writings, *kathakali* is replete with gods, demons, warriors, sages, villains and high-born ladies. To learn the classical steps of *kathakali* and its repertoire of highly stylized gestures, boys between the ages of 12 and 20 train for six years at one of several schools. Performances, which last all night long, are held throughout Kerala in temple courtyards, public spaces and private clubs.

Before going on stage, a young *kathakali* actor has his face painted green, the color that denotes the heroes of the drama. His jaw is framed by white cheekpieces of paste and paper.

The hero of a *kathakali* play, in full-skirted costume and tall crown, mimes his role to the accompaniment of a drummer. Twenty-four positions of the hands, combined in various ways, give performers a vocabulary of more than 600 words; eye movements emphasize the message conveyed by gesture.

At the Kerala State Academy of Arts, students hold the splayed stance typical of *kathakali* dance, their weight on the outside of their arched feet. From his chair, the teacher demonstrates the correct position for their hands.

1

Rose-colored sandstone buildings occupied by traders line a street in Jaipur, capital of Rajasthan. The city's 18th-century founder, Maharaja Jai Singh, laid out Jaipur's broad avenues on a rectangular grid.

was found growing wild in Assam in 1820, long after it was being cultivated in China, but the Indian tea industry did not get started until some seeds from Nepal were planted at Darjeeling, in West Bengal, in 1841. More than a century later, Assam grows 60 percent of India's crop, a distinctively strong-flavored leaf that gives body to most of the blends that Westerners drink.

West Bengal is one of the smallest states in the Indian union, but it has one of the two greatest population densities, due to its economic history and geographical position. The first part of India to come under British rule, Bengal was, in the 18th century, the source of 60 percent of all British imports from India, from silk to saltpeter. The British developed a colony on the Hooghly River into the great port of Calcutta, which became India's capital and remained so until 1912. In 1820, coal was discovered in Bengal. Soon pitshaft winding gear was poking incongruously out of the jungle, and jute mills, powered by the plentiful fuel, were multiplying. Calcutta and the other towns of the area had been transformed into thriving, machine-driven workshops, attracting migrants from all over northern India.

Bengal's population grew increasingly larger, ballooning after 1947, when the state was partitioned and the eastern half became East Pakistan. At that time, and again in 1971, when East Pakistan became Bangladesh, bloody civil war broke out within its borders. On both occasions, large numbers of refugees headed for Calcutta; many of them have stayed in the city or its surrounding area.

With a population of 9.2 million, greater Calcutta is easily the biggest city in the Commonwealth, and one of the most congested urban areas in the world. Jobs have not kept pace with the city's swelling population. Urban dilapidation and high unemployment have made for a radical population: West Bengal is one of the two states in India that regularly elect a Communist majority to their state legislature.

Like the northeast, West Bengal experiences plentiful rainfall and is, consequently, a very green part of the country. But most of northern India is extremely arid. Bihar, the state adjacent to West Bengal, is a parched plain that bakes almost white in the great summer heat. With the exception of a mining and manufacturing belt that continues from West Bengal, this is a hardscrabble tract of country where peasants till the earth with primitive instruments for a subsistence livelihood. Bihar is in some ways the most backward state, still largely run on feudal lines by substantial landowners, in spite of India's democracy.

Next to Bihar is the huge state of Uttar Pradesh, a Hindi-speaking heartland in the plain of the Ganges. Thanks to the river, which is holy to Hindus, Uttar Pradesh contains many places of pilgrimage, chief among which is the city of Varanasi. But Uttar Pradesh, like Bihar, is a very poor state. One third of its farmland is irrigated with wells or by the waters of the mighty Ganges River; the rest is dependent on unpredictable rains.

The most arid of all states is Rajasthan, much of it consisting of the great Thar desert, which extends westward beyond the Indian border into the province of Sind in Pakistan. Rajasthan is also one of India's most colorful states. It is the traditional home of a great warrior people called the Rajputs, high-caste Hindus who, like the Sikhs, invariably use the name Singh (lion) in their family titles.

In parts of Rajasthan, the camel is still the most common form of transportation outside the towns. Anyone crossing the sandy wilderness in a haze of dust kicked up by his beast encounters a series of ancient fortresses that rise dramatically from the desert floor. Within their impregnable walls are the lavish palaces owned by the Rajput princes who ruled the area—which, like Jammu and Kashmir, was semiautonomous before Independence.

Most of the former rulers still live in their strongholds, and on feast days, all the panoply of old reappears. Retainers mounted on camels and elephants caparisoned in vivid colors lead processions from the palace around the local town to the sound of trumpets, drums and pipes. The most dramatic of the Rajasthani fortifications is the town of Jaisalmer, remote in the western desert, completely encircled by battlements. The most beautiful palace is the one of Udaipur—now a hotel—which gleams with white marble and rises from the middle of a lake.

Between Rajasthan and the Arabian Sea lies the state of Gujarat, part of which before Independence consisted of numerous tiny princedoms—some of them no larger than a village—and its surrounding fields. Cotton is an important crop in the state and Ahmadabad, the state's largest city, is home to a flourishing textile industry. Gujarat is a center of the Jain religion, and Jains have strongly influenced the regional cuisine, which is entirely vegetarian and uncommonly sweet. Gujarat is the only part of India where the Asian lion is still found, a few score having survived in the Gir Forest near the southern tip of the state.

While most of Gujarat consists of featureless plain, the southern part of Madhya Pradesh, on the same latitude, rises to the Deccan plateau, the high land that occupies the middle of India's pendant shape. On this stony, infertile tract of country dotted with scrub, the sun sheds a blinding light. May temperatures of 110° F. and above are common. Madhya Pradesh is another heartland of Hindi speech and the site of one of the most celebrated of all Hindu temple complexes. Outside the village of Khajuraho, in the north of the state, cluster 20 magnificent temples to Hindu deities, all constructed between 950 and 1050 A.D. They are lavishly decorated with sculptures depicting court life, heavenly beings and erotic scenes, in friezes that are still so sharply defined that they appear to have been incised within the past five years instead of a millennium ago.

While Khajuraho's temples today are the preserve of tourists, the state of Orissa, west of Madhya Pradesh, each year mounts one of the most vital and compelling of all Hindu celebrations. In the seaside town of Puri, the image of Lord Jagganath, an incarnation of the Hindu god Vishnu, is transported down to the beach from its usual home in a temple, and returned a few days later. The journey commemorates an event in Hindu mythology and it is reenacted to the acclaim of tens of thousands of devout pilgrims who line the route. Lord Jagganath rides on a huge chariot with 16 wheels, each more than six and a half feet in diameter. In the past, it may have happened that in the mass ecstacy, pilgrims sometimes were crushed under these wheels. British misapprehension of such events gave rise to the English word "juggernaut"—a corruption of the god's name—which is used to describe an overwhelming destructive force.

Orissa is mostly a poor state with primitive agricultural methods, but it is blessed with a long coastline on the Bay

1

On the Sikkim-Nepal border, the 28,166-foot peak of Kanchenjunga — third-highest mountain in the world — rises majestically behind a herdsman's hut in the Himalayan foothills. The forces that built the Himalayas still thrust them upward, but erosion cancels the annual two inches of growth.

of Bengal and, consequently, an abundance of fish. Most of its plains and hills are covered in forest, which shelters many tribal groups.

On the opposite side of the subcontinent, the state of Maharashtra is one of the most prosperous areas of India today, particularly because of the wealth that flows in and out of its capital, Bombay. Endowed with a superb natural harbor, Bombay is a thriving center for industry of almost every kind. The city is, unquestionably, India's boom town, both in its size and in the scale of its housing and transportation problems.

Bombay, like Calcutta, attracts a great variety of people from all over India, but outside its capital, Maharashtra is culturally a fairly homogeneous state. It was defined in 1960 on the basis of the most common local language, Marathi, spoken by the warlike Maratha people who harried Mogul and British imperialists alike until well into the 19th century. The western part of the state is a narrow coastal strip separated from the Deccan plateau by a range of mountains known as the Western Ghats. They rise almost 5,000 feet above sea level and form an impressive natural barrier because of their steep seaward slopes.

Until 1947, much of the Deccan fell into the largest of all the princely states, Hyderabad. The state was peculiar in that its ruler, the nizam, was a Muslim, whereas almost all of his subjects were Hindu—just the opposite of the situation in Jammu and Kashmir. While the last of the nizams was reputed to be the richest man in the world, his state was one of the poorest in India. Today, the Marathi-speaking part of his realm has been incorporated into Maharashtra, the larger Telegu-speaking faction into Andhra Pradesh. This state remains relatively undeveloped today, although many irrigation projects that have been undertaken in the past few decades are beginning the process of converting the arid Deccan to fertility.

Of all the cultural differences in India, none is more striking than that between northerners and southerners. The transition from one zone to the other is not sudden, but the Deccan creates a natural division; Andhra Pradesh is generally southern in character, as are the other three states near the tip of the subcontinent. Language, as usual, defines the difference most clearly: southerners speak one of the Dravidian languages, which are utterly unlike the northern Aryan tongues. In general, southerners are darker skinned than people in the north of India. One theory is that the Dravidian peoples of the south may be descended from inhabitants of the Indus Valley, who were driven south by the Aryan invasion or by some natural catastrophe.

At any rate, the southerners proved resistant to the incursions of Islam, and the Mogul Empire only briefly extended into their homeland. The southerners claim, in consequence, that theirs is a purer form of Hinduism than that of the northerners. Certainly the southerners' adherence to the dietary rules of the religion is much more stringent. It is the belief of Hindus that every living creature has a soul, a soul as precious as that of a human. The practice of vegetarianism follows logically from such thinking; but in northern India, vegetarianism is more often the exception than the rule, while in the south, vegetarianism is widespread.

The southerners' choice of staple food also differs from the northern In-

1

dians'. While wheat and other cereals such as sorghum and millet are much eaten in the north, rice is the basis of any meal in the south, and the rice paddy is one of the most consistent features of the landscape in the southernmost states, Kerala and Tamil Nadu.

Men's clothing is another distinguishing feature. Women wear the sari all over India, but for men, there is no universal traditional garb. Orthodox Hindu men in northern and central India generally wear the dhoti, a sort of white skirt so amply cut that it is customary to tuck several folds between the legs to avoid tripping over them. In the south, men wear the much briefer lungi, a rectangle of cloth wrapped round the body and folded over at the waist. The lungi is usually brightly colored, often checked or flowered.

Color is also a feature of southern scenery. On temples, the figures sculpted into the external walls are painted delicately in pastel shades. Much of the southern landscape, in contrast to the bleached browns and yellows of the Ganges plain, is lush green and dappled with little reservoirs of water. These artificial ponds, which are dug by the villagers, are known all over India as tanks: The word originated in the Gujarati and Marathi languages, but the British adopted it and spread it throughout the subcontinent.

Tamil Nadu, the state below Andhra Pradesh, typifies the south in both culture and appearance. Its capital, Madras, is India's fourth-largest city, but with less than half the population of Bombay and Calcutta, it has so far escaped the worst of the problems suffered by those two metropolises. It is not nearly as congested as its rivals, nor does there seem to be as much poverty. Its streets are wider than is usual in urban India, and its public transportation system does not look as if it were about to collapse after too much hard labor on behalf of too many passengers.

Karnataka, the third southern state, contains one of India's most dynamic cities and another that seems almost untouched by time. Bangalore is a bustling center of high-technology industry, including aircraft manufacture; Mysore, once the capital of a princely state, has one of the most opulent palaces in the country, which is still a fairyland of light every Sunday evening, glittering with thousands of lamps, as it was in the days when the maharaja's word was law. Mysore's specialty is manufacturing incense. All over the city, there are workshops where bamboo slivers are coated with perfumed powder, and the air is fragrant with the scent of sandalwood, jasmine and rose. Karnataka provides most of the world's supply of sandalwood, and in Mysore, there are many artisans who carve the aromatic wood into ornamental boxes or statues of deities.

Kerala, the long strip of country bordering the Arabian Sea to the south of Karnataka, has long been famous for an equally exotic set of products: spices. This was the Malabar coast, which attracted first the Portuguese and later the British to buy the pepper, cloves and ginger that made their monotonous winter diet palatable. It is a palmy land of lush backwaters and rice paddies, where out-of-town travel more often means taking a diesel-engined ferryboat than a bus. Today, Kerala has a considerable industrial base at Cochin, where there is a modern seaport and a shipyard. Otherwise, its economy is still based primarily on spices, along with fish, rice and coconuts. Many of Kerala's young men have taken to working

Two workmen paint traffic markers on the Rajpath, the principal avenue of India's capital, New Delhi. Beyond the red sandstone Secretariat, the thoroughfare leads to the domed residence of the Indian president — an edifice completed in 1929 to accommodate the British viceroy.

Accompanied by a woman spectator, a cricketer rests before taking his turn at bat. The carefully tended field belongs to the exclusive Calcutta Cricket Club; founded by the British in 1792, it is the oldest cricket club outside the United Kingdom.

for a few years in the oil-rich Gulf States: The money they send home buys motorbikes, cars and houses.

Socially, Kerala is unusual in several ways. It has a greater than average mixture of religions, including a Christian community—as old as any in Europe—accounting for 18 percent of the population. The Hindus of Kerala—the majority in the state—adhere to a strict version of the code that keeps different castes apart. One rule, only recently abandoned, stated that a low-caste person may not come within 96 paces of someone from the highest castes.

Surprisingly, given the hierarchic nature of Hindu society in Kerala, the state has the highest literacy rate in India—nearly 70 percent, compared with 36 percent in India as a whole. One explanation is that the Maharaja of Travancore, who ruled much of what is now Kerala until Independence, was an enlightened man who encouraged the dissemination of learning among his people. Another is that the Christian community has always shown a strong commitment to education, and the Hindus were obliged to share that attitude in order not to be outstripped economically and politically.

Kerala's other claim to fame is that it produced the world's first democratically elected Communist government, in 1957. Communists have been in power in the state for most most of the intervening period. The radicalism of the people seems to stem more from their political awareness, through reading books and newspapers, than from desperation, for there is less destitution here than in many parts of India. Kerala is the most crowded state in India, with 1,700 people packed into each square mile, compared with 575 in India as a whole. Yet enough food is produced for everyone, thanks to the state's abundant and reliable rainfall.

With a large portion of India's population dependent on the land, rainfall crucially affects lives. The monsoon, the seasonally varying wind of south Asia, brings the rain. Each year, mil-

1

lions wait and watch, anxious and hopeful, as the monsoon crosses the land. They follow radio and newspaper reports of its progress with intense interest. It is an age-old anxiety.

Most parts of India are blessed with only one spell of rain annually, and the early part of the year is dry throughout the subcontinent. January is India's coldest month, with temperatures below 60° F. in Delhi and ice forming on Kashmir's Dal Lake. But the temperature rises sharply in March and April, and by May, it frequently exceeds 100° F. in the plain of the Ganges. The people ache for the rains.

Then at last, with great thunderstorms, the monsoon breaks and drenched farmers laugh with relief. The rain-bearing wind comes from the southwest and reaches southern India at the end of May. Gradually, over the next few weeks, the wind makes its way up the subcontinent; Kashmir's first visitation by the monsoon does not happen until July. In a normal year, every part of the country should look forward to three months of this rain, which falls torrentially for a few hours, then stops while everything steams in the sun, before the rain continues where it left off. But in some years, the monsoon expires before rain reaches the northwest in any quantity, with disastrous consequences for the local farmers. And some years, the Thar desert receives no rain at all.

Scarcely ever does the monsoon fail to irrigate a tract of the country to the south and east of a line extending from Goa (below Bombay) to Patna (in Bihar). More often than not, the extreme south is visited by additional rain, borne by a northeast monsoon, between the months of October and December, when the monsoon season has ended in the rest of India. It is this bonus of rain that keeps the south—especially Kerala—so lush and green.

The transformation of India's rivers from one season to the next is phenomenal. By the end of May, a week or two before the rainy season begins, the Ganges has sunk so low in its passage across Uttar Pradesh and Bihar that it is scarcely flowing at all; at Kanpur, near the center of Uttar Pradesh, it is quite easy for people to wade from bank to bank. Within a week of the monsoon starting, the sluggish stream has become a raging torrent 3,000 feet wide, and getting wider by the day. For a short spell after the rains end for the year, the swollen Ganges rolls majestically across northern India. Then gradually, imperceptibly, the water level lowers day by day until, nine months later, the river is restored to full vigor by the next monsoon.

Wherever the monsoon fails, crops die for lack of water and whole populations are threatened. In 1943, a famine in Bengal killed a documented 1.5 million people—and perhaps twice that number died. Admittedly, the 1943 famine was one of the last real natural catastrophes, and India is now moving toward rudimentary efficiency in warehousing supplies. But hardship and death are never out of sight; when the monsoon appears on schedule, the specter of famine disappears temporarily, but there is usually disaster for some people in floods that sweep whole villages away, drowning humans and animals by the hundreds.

To most outsiders, the precariousness of life in India is epitomized by the poverty to be seen in its cities. In Calcutta and Bombay especially, but to a lesser degree in every Indian community of size, the beggar is a customary

Groups of turbaned men camp with their camels at the annual fair near the village of Pushkar in Rajasthan. Held during a full moon in October or early November, the fair draws thousands of villagers from the surrounding region for a week of livestock dealing and religious festivities.

1

sight upon the streets. Women rush up to strangers and almost thrust their sleeping babies into their arms as they ask for money; children ambush their quarry with upheld palms and piteously tearful cries of "No mamma, no papa." Some beggars are dreadfully mutilated, lending weight to suspicions that evil men sometimes deliberately cripple infants and thereafter live off the income these poor children earn by engaging the compassion of passersby. Generally speaking, however, the typical Indian beggar is simply undernourished, ill clad, without possessions or permanent residence. He is likely to live with his family on the streets or in vacant lots, cooking his meager supplies of food on an open fire.

Those lucky enough to have found a job in a city seem scarcely better off. Millions live in the kind of pestilential tenements that the Western world began to abandon in the middle of the 19th century. Overcrowding is acute; an entire family will deem itself lucky to have a single room to itself.

Yet for all its difficulties, city life is often preferable to life in the country, where the vagaries of the weather are compounded by an acute shortage of land. India was a crowded country at Independence; since then, as a result of a high birth rate and decreasing mortality, the population has more than doubled. Most people living in the countryside are now without enough land to subsist, and in a village that is overpopulated, there may be literally no way for a landless family to earn a living. During the past few decades, there has been a growing movement of peasants to the cities from the rural areas that fail to sustain them. Sometimes, men come to the cities on their own and work there for years at a time, sending part of their pay back to their wives and families in the home village each month by money order.

In this country where poverty is so evident and widespread, fantastic wealth is enjoyed by a small elite. The riches of the rajas and maharajas were diminished after Independence, when they surrendered their local sovereignties and treasure hoards in exchange for allowances that were paid annually by the government. The payments were abolished in 1970, along with the titles. But many of the former princes are still figures of considerable property: They were never obliged to surrender their palaces and still maintain luxurious abodes and family heirlooms in an extravagant style—the like of which is known to only a handful of monarchs in Europe today. India's wealthiest industrialists live in an equally sumptuous manner.

Such contrasts are deeply disturbing to the sensibilities of Westerners. Some wonder why it is that Communism has gained no more than a small foothold in Indian political life. The answer lies partly in a strong social fabric, bound by tradition. India is still a profoundly religious country and the Hindu faith deems it a virtue to come to terms with one's lot, no matter how lowly.

Resentments do sometimes flare up in bouts of communal violence. However, considering all the tinder for conflict, India is more notable for its tolerance than its rifts. Most of the time, the rich coexist peacefully with the poor, Muslims with Hindus, northerners with southerners, imperial relics with national institutions. India even achieves the feat of abiding in several centuries at once. The acceptance of different stages of civilization is an old tradition: Tribal peoples have long lived peaceably next to Hindu villagers, and India's foreign rulers made few attempts to stamp out native customs.

Today, the contrast between ancient and modern lifestyles is even more acute. India, long an industrial nation, is becoming a force to be reckoned with in computer and space research: It has designed and launched its own satellites for remote sensing and mass communication. In the same cities where beggars work the streets like figures from a painting by Brueghel, there thrives a highly advanced technology to

Three young men scour an elephant with coconut husks in a roadside stream in Kerala. Elephants — powerful and intelligent work animals — are important to logging operations in south India and expect a refreshing daily bath as a reward for their labors.

During a monsoon shower in Kerala, villagers are ferried across one of the palm-fringed backwaters that wind behind the coastal town of Quilon. More than 1,000 miles of inland waterways constitute the state's main arteries of communication.

rival anything in the West. Meanwhile, the old ways continue.

Anyone who visits Bombay and takes a boat trip to Elephanta Island experiences a perfect example of India's astonishing time spectrum. The launches depart not far from an imposing arch, the Gateway of India, built by the British to commemmorate the landing there of King George V in 1911. The tourist boat crosses the great harbor, full of merchant vessels from all over the globe, to the island named by the Portuguese after a great stone elephant that they found when they arrived in the 16th century.

The animal was carved in the eighth century. During the same period, a series of vast caves dedicated to the god Shiva and his consort were hewn from the living rock of the island and intricately sculpted inside. In one of these shrines stands a chest-high stone carving that represents the conjoining of male and female organs. The *yoni-linga* is the symbol of Hinduism's most forceful injunction to multiply. For 12 centuries, Hindu women hoping to have children, especially boys, have gone to Elephanta to pray at the *yoni-linga*. It still happens every day.

Those traveling to the holy island nowadays will notice other strange shapes standing below a hillside across a short stretch of sparkling water. These large, silver domes, gleaming in the sunlight, contain India's first nuclear reactor. Atomic energy and the still-potent shrine of Lord Shiva and his consort are separated by only a short stretch of Bombay's harbor.

Few places on earth embrace such juxtapositions. India is a land where anything is possible, where fantasies are almost a matter of course, where all the flavors are strong. □

An actor wears the costume of Ravana, villain of the Sanskrit epic the Ramayana. The poem tells of the heroic battle of King Rama — an incarnation of the god Vishnu — to free his abducted wife, Sita, from Ravena. The tale is enacted each autumn all over north India to commemorate Rama's birth.

A SANCTIFIED SOCIAL ORDER

No visitor to India can fail to perceive that he has come to a deeply religious society. Within an hour of his arriving, he or she is bound to catch sight of someone whose forehead has been painted with white ash or with colored powder. Most likely there will be two or three horizontal lines across the brow, or some vertical marks starting where the nose ends and the forehead begins. The horizontal lines signify that the wearer is a devotee of the god Shiva; the vertical marks indicate that the wearer is a disciple of the deity Vishnu. The visitor has encountered his first ardent Hindu, and for the rest of his time on the subcontinent, such people will vividly color his impressions of India. In a country where all religions are practiced assiduously, there is no doubt that Hinduism is far and away the dominant creed, and its philosophies touch every aspect of daily life.

It is one of the oldest of the world's great religions; only Judaism has a claim to greater antiquity. The origins of Hinduism are believed to lie in the arrival of the Aryans on the subcontinent in approximately 1500 B.C. The Aryans, who came from central Asia, brought their own gods with them, and as they settled across the plains and forests of northern India, they assimilated into their religion the deities of the land's indigenous peoples. The result is a vast pantheon, most of whose members can appear in many guises. The same god sometimes appears as a man, sometimes as a woman, for gods possess aspects of both genders.

During their first two millennia in India, the Aryans memorized a verbal form of sacred literature known as the Vedas, a word whose singular means "knowledge." There are four Vedas—Rig Veda, Yajur Veda, Sama Veda and Atharva Veda—and each Veda has four sections: Samhita, Brahmanas, Aranyakas and Upanishads. The oldest of the Vedas is the Rig Veda—"the Veda of praise"—which contains a collection of 1,017 hymns addressed to the various gods of the Aryans. Most of these hymns were written down before 100 B.C.

The prose sections of the Vedas, the Brahmanas, codified the rituals and prayers of the Brahmins—the priests of the Aryans. The Upanishads, which have dominated Indian philosophy and religion for almost 3,000 years, are the concluding parts of the Vedas. They are discourses between teachers and students, not unlike the discourses of ancient Greek philosophy. The Epic Period, which originated about the sixth century before Christ, saw the composition of the Puranas, which are essentially the history of the Aryan race and its relationship with the gods.

The two most famous Puranic epics are the Ramayana and the Mahabharata, both mythologizing events that took place between 1000 and 700 B.C. While the Ramayana simply recounts a sequence of heroic adventures—many

2

Outside a temple in Tamil Nadu, a priest honors a cow and her calf with garlands and offerings of flower petals and saffron. Although some cows are kept by temples, most of the sacred animals wander the streets, dependent on the faithful for sustenance.

of them with moral undertones—the Mahabharata interweaves ideas about cosmology, statecraft, philosophy and the science of war into its stories of the deeds of gods and men. It is believed to be the longest poem in any language. By far the best-known section of the epic now is the sequence of 18 chapters entitled Bhagavad Gita, "the song of the Lord," in which the god Krishna expounds on such subjects as duty, asceticism and devotion. The Gita is partly memorized by many Hindus, who recite portions of the verses at prayer each day. If the Hindu religion has an equivalent of Christianity's New Testament, it is this.

An Aryan might be startled by some changes that have taken place in his religion since Vedic times. He would find that many of the gods he worshipped most faithfully have been forgotten by modern Hindus; some have been considerably demoted, others surprisingly elevated. Indra, the great war god of the Aryans, has become a rain god, and Varuna, once ruler of heaven and earth and the oceans, is now little worshipped. Today, Hinduism's vast complexity of gods is dominated by a divine triumvirate consisting of Brahma, Shiva and Vishnu; in Vedic times these were all minor figures.

Of these three deities, Brahma is in a sense the foremost, being the creator of the world. Yet he occupies a strangely remote position in the Hindu pantheon, where the tendency is to personalize deities as much as possible. In all of India, only one important temple—at Pushkar in Rajasthan—is dedicated to Brahma. Vishnu is the ruler of the world and stands straightforwardly for the preservation of life. Shiva is a god of paradoxes, representing in one deity both destruction and reproduction, man and woman, wild hunter and sage teacher of arts and sciences. As a male, he can be a terrible and frightening presence, or he can be an admirable prince among gods.

In his female aspect, Shiva comes in several guises: the mild, maternal figures of Parvati and Uma, the strong Durga, or the vengeful Kali, perhaps the most frightening being in the divine scheme of things. She is usually represented as a black figure, with a necklace of skulls, one of her multiple hands holding a bloody knife, another grasping a freshly severed head.

The Western mind is easily bewildered by Hinduism's habit of invoking Shiva, and many of its other deities, under different names, sometimes because of different regional titles, sometimes because of different incarnations. There are scores of permutations of the primary gods alone, to which must be added an infinite number of lesser gods that often have local appeal.

Despite this plethora of divinities, the philosophy of Hinduism is fundamentally monotheistic, a fact that Westerners often find hard to grasp. All Hindu gods are aspects of the supreme spirit Brahman—not to be confused with the creator Brahma—who is the ultimate principle existing in all things. Brahman's infinity, Hindus maintain, cannot be comprehended by humans, so they have created myriad manageable forms of the deity to worship.

Every large village boasts several temples, dedicated to different gods, but many Hindus feel no compulsion to visit them regularly. Most people worship at home, in a corner of the house furnished with a poster of a deity or a brass or sandalwood image. They address an occasional prayer to the major figures in the pantheon, but on the whole, they reserve their devotions for one particular god, not necessarily an important one, to whom they pray every day. The main family deity is inherited patrilineally; in addition, some members of a family, particularly the women, may direct many of their prayers to another god who engages their affections. A lot of women are ardent devotees of Krishna, a handsome and romantic incarnation of the god Vishnu.

The everyday pattern of worship is frequently varied by Hindu festivals. In autumn, the five-day celebration known as Diwali is chiefly dedicated to the goddess Lakshmi, giver of wealth. Merchants are particularly zealous in keeping Diwali, which marks the beginning of the Hindu financial year. In spring, in northern India, there is tremendous celebration to symbolize the downfall of the evil Holika. This festival, called Holi, extends over several days, starting one evening with bonfires and continuing through the next day when young people fling brightly colored powders and water over one another—and anyone else who happens to come along. Holi is an occasion to let off steam: It licenses servants to insult their masters for a day, and wives their husbands.

In Bengal, each October sees the celebration of Durga Puja, when lavish and lovingly created images of the goddess are set up in every village and town. Prayers are said before these images for a week, while everyone enjoys the fun of the fair. Then, on the last day, the elaborate representations of Durga, made of vividly painted papier-mâché and clay, are carried to the nearest river, to float away out of sight and eventually to sink.

Everybody takes part in such festi-

vals; for the more devout, a natural step at some stage in life is to take a pilgrimage to a holy shrine. One of the most important temples is in Madurai, in central Tamil Nadu, where, according to Hindu mythology, Shiva married an incarnation of Parvati. The temple is flanked by four enormous towers, each one carved with thousands of gaily colored mythological figures. The temple's outer walls enclose a total area of 15 acres, and much of it is roofed. Entering it is like stepping into a small walled city.

On any day of any week, it is estimated that up to 10,000 pilgrims make their way to the temple. Immediately inside the entrances, they encounter small bazaars selling incense, flowers, idols and other religious bric-a-brac. Two elephants flank a corridor, their hides decorated with colored chalk. At the dozens of shrines within, Hindus busy themselves with their devotions. An attendant stands beside a tub of water in which dozens of globes of *ghee*—clarified butter—are floating. Because the cow is sacred to Hindus, its products have a sacramental quality. Pilgrims buy the tiny pats of butter to flick at a huge statue of Kali in pious enthusiasm. At little alcoves along the many corridors in the temple, various gods and goddesses wear garlands of marigolds and other blooms that have been strung together; and near each alcove is a steel box with a slit in the top for the donation of rupees.

The greatest destination of all pilgrimages in India is the city of Varanasi—also known as Benares—on the Ganges. Many pilgrims are very old; they come in the hope that they will die before they go back home. Hindus fervently believe that to die in Varanasi, to be cremated there and to have one's ashes cast upon the holy Ganges River, is the greatest blessing one can attain. According to Hindu theology, the soul inhabits not just one but a series of physical forms during its passage

2

through the cosmos, until it reaches its final goal of liberation from the endless cycle of birth, death and rebirth. But by dying in Varanasi, which is a bridge between this world and the next, one can cleanse oneself of all immoral actions, thus obtaining release for the soul from the perpetual cycle and burden of life.

Even those who never make the pilgrimage to Varanasi can affect their soul's future by their deeds and misdeeds. A good life may be rewarded by rebirth as a Brahmin, a bad life by reappearance in the lowest orders of human society, or even as a quadruped, a reptile or an insect. Consequently, a person's position in life is seen as a reflection of acts committed in an earlier existence. Destitution and high position alike have been earned.

The Hindu doctrine of the transmigration of souls provides a powerful rationale for India's unique social system—the division of the population into a hierarchy of castes. In this life, one cannot escape from the caste one was born into, but Hindus see no injustice in such a fate—it is the outcome of the way one has lived one's past life.

Although the scriptures accord women and women's role great respect, women have traditionally occupied a low position in Indian society. They are submissive adjuncts of their husbands, and they generally lead a restricted and laborious life. But once again, religion can be used to justify their status. Birth into the so-called inferior sex is no more a matter of chance than birth into one of the lower castes—it is the legacy of misdeeds in a previous existence.

Religion and the immutable social order are interwoven with the Hindu concept of virtue. A good life—one that will lead to a good rebirth—is a question of performing the duties allotted to one's station. While Hindus are charitable—they give generously to beggars, for example—because of their adherence to a universal code of ethics, this commitment does not lead to social reform. Its imperatives are, rather, bowing to the restrictions that are imposed by one's caste and sex.

Although the Hindu religion provides a rationale for the caste system, pragmatic considerations no doubt brought it into existence in the first place. A precursor of the caste system seems to have existed in the Indus Valley civilization more than 3,000 years ago: Workers in different trades lived in different sections of a city, and elaborate facilities for washing and bathing discovered by archeologists suggest that the citizens may have shared modern-day Hindus' fervor for ritual cleanliness. But caste in something like its modern form first appeared in the Aryan society that superceded that of the Indus Valley. By keeping different sections of the population apart, the embryonic caste system promoted the peaceful coexistence of the Aryan invaders and the indigenous people. Caste has survived to the present day partly because it enables a huge and heterogeneous population to live in moderately peaceful proximity.

The Vedic literature of the Aryans divided the population into four broad categories—*varnas*—and a fifth classification for those who did not belong to the other four. The upper categories were composed of the pale-skinned Aryans themselves, and the lower ones were made up of the older inhabitants of India, the Dravidians, who had darker complexions.

Westerners often equate the *varnas* with castes—India's closed societies,

Shiva lifts his consort, Sati, from her pyre.

Images of Hinduism's millions of gods and goddesses are ubiquitous. Elaborate murals adorn temples, simple chalk drawings brighten paving stones. The pictures are more than mere aids to the human imagination in its acts of devotion: If an immortal's image is executed in accordance with the canons of divine beauty, the god himself is held to inhabit it.

The iconography of Hindu art was established some 2,000 years ago. The features of the various gods are similar: Both sexes have large eyes, full lips and luxuriant hair. Frequently, only clothing or weaponry distinguishes a certain divinity. Gods are sometimes shown with multiple appendages to emphasize their superhuman attributes. Shiva is one of the deities portrayed at times with several arms, denoting power. Brahma, the creator, occasionally has four heads, allowing him to gaze lustfully at his bride, Saraswati, from different angles.

PORTRAYALS OF THE DEITIES

The elephant-headed Ganesh, god of luck and success, sits with Krishna, god of love.

The monkey god Hanuman protects wrestlers.

The warrior goddess Durga, fierce guardian against the threat of evil, kills a demon.

Snakes and skulls garland Kali, goddess of death.

2

which marry only among themselves and which avoid contact with other castes. But in fact the *varnas* are only broad groupings, within each of which there are many castes.

The four *varnas* still determine the basic structure of Hindu society. In descending order of merit, and in accordance with their original occupations, they are the Brahmins (priests and men of learning), the Kshatriyas (rulers and warriors), the Vaishyas (the merchants and landholders) and the Shudras (servants and artisan work force). Girls as well as boys inherit their father's *varna.*

Beneath the four *varnas,* there has always existed a substantial segment of Indian society—approximately 15 percent—known since ancient times as *niravasita,* meaning "excluded." These are the Untouchables, whom the great 20th-century spiritual leader, Mahatma Gandhi, tried to dignify by giving the name of Harijans, "children of god," and whom the Indian government refers to as the "Scheduled Castes." The Constitution of India, with its intensely democratic ideals, does not recognize the caste system and specifically forbids discrimination against Untouchables. But beliefs and customs developed over thousands of years have proved extremely resistant to official decree.

An important fact of life for any faithful Hindu has been that only if he belongs to one of the first three *varnas*—excluding the Shudras—is he in theory entitled to hear, learn or recite the Vedas. Since the Vedas are still regarded as the source of all revelation for Hindus, the exclusion effectively cuts off the Shudras (and also, of course, the Untouchables) from the mainstream of religious activity.

Only if a Hindu boy is born Brahmin, Kshatriya or Vaishya will he be allowed to take part in the initiation ceremony that will introduce him to religious life. Brahmin priests perform the ritual over the boy between the ages of eight and 12 years. At the climax of the ceremony, the child is invested with a sacred thread, which is strung over his left shoulder and under his right arm, that he must wear for the rest of his life. Once a boy has undergone this initiation—which may be compared to the confirmation of a Christian child, or the bar or bas mitzvah of a young Jew—he is known, in Hindu terminology, as one of the "twice-born."

In the 20th century, the old occupations related to the four *varnas* are often irrelevant. What has remained static, however, is the position of the Brahmins—some 6 percent of India's Hindu population—as exclusive practitioners of the priestly function. Many of them nowadays do not exercise their priestly role. But Brahmins alone may conduct rituals, wherever these are required; only they may have charge of Hindu temples, ordering all ceremonies and receiving all donations. It is not necessary for them to be well educated, even in a religious sense, to assume the duties and privileges of a Hindu priest. It is sufficient that they have been born Brahmin, men who can automatically exist on a different plane from everyone else if they so choose.

The Brahmins, the other three *varnas* and the Untouchables represent only the first level of demarcation in an enormously complex society. The compartments that really matter in daily life in India are the castes—which developed some time after the Vedic period. Each of the four *varnas* may contain many hundreds or thousands of castes, and there is a hierarchy of castes even among the Untouchables.

One can rarely be sure of a person's caste from his appearance, though skin color and details of dress and behavior provide clues. In the villages, where three quarters of the population live, everyone's caste is known. Even in the city, where anonymity is possible, social life revolves around the extended family, and to renounce one's caste means losing one's connections.

Caste boundaries are defined primarily by type of work, by location and by language. So it is that a potter will belong to a different caste from a stonemason in the same village, and a Rajasthani blacksmith to a different caste from a blacksmith in Tamil Nadu. Caste applies equally to men and women: The blacksmith's daughter, like her brothers, inherits her father's caste.

Besides language, location and occupation, so many additional factors can subdivide a group of people into different castes that the question Westerners are wont to ask—How many castes are there in India?—is quite impossible to answer. No realistic attempt could be made to count them all.

In a single community, however, it is possible to enumerate the castes represented. Some Indian villages are populated exclusively by a single caste, but a much more common pattern is for a village of a few thousand people to have representatives of two or three dozen castes. Among them, they can perform all the tasks regularly done in the village, making it an interdependent and autonomous community. Service relationships between families of different castes are handed down from one generation to the next. Some castes may be represented in the village by only one or two families. Since marriage is vir-

At the confluence of the Ganges and Yamuna rivers in Allahabad, disciples bear a holy man aloft during the Kumbha-mela, a ritual bathing festival held every three years along one of India's sacred rivers. Every 12 years, when the stars are in a rare conjunction, millions of the faithful attend.

tually always within the caste, young people from the underrepresented castes are obliged to seek marriage partners from other villages.

Even today, most Indians, as a matter of course, take up the work that their caste has allotted them. Often they have no choice: It would be most unusual for a villager to dream of trespassing on the traditional occupation of another caste in his community. However, education and modern technology have created opportunities—which never existed before—for breaking out of caste roles. The multiplicity of new trades and skills for which there is no time-hallowed caste are often open to all enterprising Indians. For instance, in practically every village these days can be found someone skilled in ad hoc repairs to motorcycles and trucks, and the self-styled auto mechanic may come from any caste. Factories in towns and cities also bring together male and female laborers from a mixture of castes.

But even if two factory workers from different castes get to know each other, the intimacy very rarely extends to marriage. Young people are expected to accept an arranged marriage with someone from their own caste, even in Indian cities. Only the wealthy can afford to ignore these constraints. Among the educated, there is much discussion over the question of loosening the shackles of caste and marrying for love. But even among such people, bold words are more common than actions. A surprising proportion of apparently thoroughly Westernized Indians fall back into their inherited caste positions when it comes to the question of marriage.

Newspaper advertisements are often the means by which city dwellers find suitable spouses for their children. Oc-

2

casionally, advertisers will note that "caste is no bar" but much more often they will specify, in addition to such qualities as youth, domesticity and ambition, the caste and the skin color of the potential bride or groom.

In villages, breaking the mold is still virtually unheard of. If a couple took the extraordinary step of marrying outside their castes, they would almost certainly leave home. However, even in a new environment, it would be difficult for them to conceal what they had done, and their children would have a hard time fitting into society.

If the village contains people whose religion is other than Hinduism—for example, Muslims—the Hindus would think of them as belonging to a separate caste. They may indeed form more than one additional caste. A peculiarity of India is that, although caste has no part in the dogma of any religion but Hinduism, the concept has to differing extents pervaded other religions, as converts from Hinduism retained their social traditions. Anthropologists detect caste distinctions of a sort among Muslims, Christians, Sikhs and Jains.

In any community, there is a strict hierarchy of castes known to everyone. Yet this hierarchy is not fixed for all time. Over the years, certain social groups can rise or fall in the esteem of others and consequently in their relationships with other groups. A caste, or a section of a caste, may sink if its members collectively fail to adhere to caste rituals. A caste determined to rise socially may give itself a new name, take on a new trade or impose on itself stricter rules of behavior—possibly all three. Thus the Telis, traditionally a caste of oil pressers in northern India, have boosted themselves in the past few generations by becoming small grocers and shop owners. In a Rajasthani village, the members of the Shudra caste of Yadows—stonemasons—have steadily risen over the past five generations by subtly altering their attire and daily habits to set themselves apart from other humble castes.

When there is movement, it is always

Mass-produced illustrations from the lives of Krishna and Shiva paper a Hindu domestic shrine. In ceremonies held three times a day, the heads of the household ring the brass bell on the table, summoning Krishna to enter his flute-playing image.

the movement of an entire caste. For the individual, there can be no movement from one caste to another by marriage or any other means—only the ostracism that will follow if he defies any of the caste conventions and makes himself outcaste, cutting himself off from Hinduism altogether.

In the end, the conventions of caste depend on what is considered to be pure, and what impure. That is the social foundation of the Hindu religion. It touches life at every turn. It is the perpetual preoccupation of every one of Hinduism's believers. It provides the logic behind the separation of one caste from another, so that contact is kept to the absolute essential.

To the Western mind, the intricate rules governing purity and contamination can seem bizarre and frequently contradictory. Inconsistencies are inevitable in a vast society that has evolved over a long time span, but the system does have its own logic. High castes are seen as intrinsically pure, though they are capable of temporary defilement. On the other hand, the lower castes are indelibly stained, no matter what they do. Yet they can be defiled still further, so everybody, except the very lowest orders of society, takes at least some precautions against pollution.

Contamination can be canceled out, but only by laborious rites. Usually the procedure involves bathing, perhaps fasting, and prayer. If a man is not sure what ritual is appropriate for a rare occurrence—adultery with a woman of lower caste, for example—he will call in a Brahmin to supervise and instruct him. Occasionally, a Hindu may perform some impure act and try to get away with it. If that happens, other members of his caste will intervene to insist that he purge himself correctly. Their overwhelmingly powerful sanction is the threat to exclude him from the community.

Food and drink may transmit contamination from one person to another and necessitate a cleansing ritual. Fire, however, is a purifying agent, so a high-caste person may buy raw food from an Untouchable, provided the food is to be cooked. What he must ensure is that the cook is of his own caste or a higher caste. One practical result of this injunction is that many Brahmins have become cooks, since anyone can accept food that they have prepared. Food fried in clarified butter presents less of a problem than boiled food, because the sacramental quality of cow's milk purifies what would otherwise be unacceptable: A Brahmin may therefore eat fried sweets bought from a professional confectioner belonging to a somewhat lower caste.

Direct physical contact with a person is also polluting. Westerners must learn not to extend their hands automatically when being introduced to Indians. Politeness may compel the Indian to shake the proffered hand but he will then be saddled with the obligation of taking a ritual bath. In the south, the concept of pollution by bodily contact in the past extended to contamination by proximity, and the mere sight of an Untouchable would have been sufficient to defile a high-caste Hindu. But in cities, it is impossible to avoid such contact. Most Hindu city dwellers are reconciled to the necessity of jostling against all kinds of people of unknown caste as they struggle for a seat on the bus or in a theater. They lead a double life, following the rules of purity and pollution in the home, but ignoring them at work and in the street.

Impure people do not constitute the only sources of defilement. Some foods are polluting in themselves. Foremost among them, because of the cow's sanctity, is beef. Some Untouchable castes do partake of it, but the very idea of consuming beef would horrify most Hindus. Other foods are taboo only to high castes or to castes in certain parts of the country. Thus, many Hindus in the north will quite happily eat lamb

At the Minakshi Temple in Madurai, Tamil Nadu, a painted beast surveys lofty gateways whose carvings portray the Hindu pantheon. The 17th-century shrine's complex of halls and courts reflects its early role as meeting place, theater and school, as well as temple.

2

and chicken, while in the south their coreligionists will insist on a vegetarian diet. Influenced many centuries ago by Buddhist doctrines condemning alcohol, most high castes never touch wine or hard liquor.

Even if the foods consumed are pure, the very act of eating is considered by Hindus to be defiling. So are urination, defecation, menstruation and sexual intercourse, as well as contact with birth and death. Each caste has its own variation on the rituals that must be performed in order to cancel out the effects of these agents of impurity.

Death brings with it the most tortuous purification rituals; for until a body is cremated, the soul is trapped within it; the earthbound, restless soul is a source of great spiritual danger to the living. Because of their exposure to the peril, the close relatives of a dead Brahmin are impure for 10 days after the death, Kshatriyas 12, Vaishyas 15, Shudras 30. During those periods, the relatives of the dead person are treated by all others as though they were untouchable. No one else to whom Hindu caste matters will have anything to do with them. Thus it is usually only the immediate family who attends the funeral ceremonies and the cremation of the body according to Hindu rites. It is true that large numbers of people attended the services for Mahatma Gandhi, for India's first Prime Minister Jawaharlal Nehru, and for Nehru's daughter, Indira Gandhi: The huge crowds were an indication of the distance India has traveled from the strictest orthodoxies of Hinduism. These were special cases, however, and death retains its taboo.

The orthodox attitude toward the cow best exemplifies the Hindu response to the uncleanliness of death. In life, the cow is regarded with such devotion that it has become a notable inconvenience in urban India. Droves of cows can sometimes be seen wandering down the middle of main roads in the big cities, compelling motorists to take evasive action. Shopkeepers—whose premises, more often than not, open directly onto the street without benefit of glazed windows—are accustomed to cows browsing through their goods with impunity. The vendor dares do no more than wave his arms at the beast in the hope of driving it off. If he took more vigorous action and some officious Brahmin spotted him, he might well have more trouble on his hands than the nuisance provided by the cow.

It has been a sacred animal since Vedic times, probably because herds of cattle represented the most precious wealth of the Aryan tribes: The cows provided not only labor and transportation but dung for fertilizer and heat, as well as milk. At one time, Aryans certainly sacrificed cattle to the gods and ate the meat, but later, piety led them to deny themselves this pleasure. The chief Hindu sins are the murder of a Brahmin and the killing of a cow. Indeed, veneration for the cow is a more constant feature of Indian life than respect for the Brahmin.

Yet the moment the cow dies, it is transformed from a creature whose life is extraordinarily precious into merely a carcass. In Indian society, it is the Untouchables who perform all the most degrading tasks—those that inevitably involve defilement—and among the most characteristic occupations of Untouchables are the disposal of dead cattle, the tanning of their skins, and any work that involves contact with cowhide. The Pariyar caste in Tamil Nadu, for example, furnishes the drummers for the state's many village bands. The job is one that can be done only by Untouchables because the drum skins are made of cowhide. The name of the caste long ago entered the English language as "pariah."

The great excluded mass of Untouchables is as riddled with caste as the four *varnas* of Hindu society. There can be several castes of Harijans in the same district, and they will maintain similar rules of conduct for avoiding defilement among themselves as those that exist in the upper echelons of Hinduism. In Uttar Pradesh, the Dhobis—the laundrymen who handle dirty linen—are regarded as untouchable by the Untouchable caste of Dom, who are basket weavers, but in addition perform the defiling task of cremating dead bodies. The sweepers, because they have to clear dirt and refuse from the streets, probably come lowest of all in most Hindus' scheme of things. As a democratic gesture, Mahatma Gandhi repeatedly performed the task of a sweeper. (He was a member of a grocer caste in the Vaishya *varna*.) Such was the force of his personality that huge crowds followed him—but they would not go so far as to touch him. The Hindu religion is an extremely fastidious social order.

In accordance with its rules, Untouchables have traditionally been segregated in dwellings situated some distance away from those of other members of the village. In most parts of the country, they have not been allowed to use the same wells as others, and they have been forbidden access to most Hindu places of worship.

Even today, with the law on their side, the Scheduled Castes in practice are denied equal status with other Hindus. A survey of 1,155 villages throughout India in the late 1970s found that in

54 percent of the villages, Untouchables were not permitted to use the public well. In 71 percent of the villages, they were refused entry to public temples. In over 40 percent of the villages, Untouchables were turned away from local cafés and barbershops. Very few cases have been brought under the Untouchability (Offenses) Act; and few of those have been decided in favor of the Untouchables.

Nowadays, the Scheduled Castes have, in theory at least, been granted many special privileges. They are entitled to free schooling, while other castes generally have to pay a nominal sum for their children's lessons. Untouchables are also assigned a large number of reserved places in universities and colleges, reserved positions in the civil service and seats in Parliament. Often, Untouchable families cannot take advantage of this affirmative action. Free schooling, for example, means that a child must have good clothes and that he can no longer help in the fields. But a fraction of the Untouchable population has benefitted from these measures and prospered—thereby angering other Hindus.

The Harijan who offends other Hindus is likely to be severely treated, notwithstanding the fact that the laws of the land are on his side. In the 1980s, high-caste would-be university students who are poor have frequently rioted in protest against quotas for Untouchables. Beatings and worse—sometimes provoked by jealousy of a Harijan's upward mobility, but more often by anger at quotas based on caste rather than need—are common. A result of this mistreatment is that many millions of Harijans have converted to other faiths in the decades since Independence, hoping thereby to encounter less discrimination. In the states of Maharashtra and Madhya Pradesh, most of the conversions have been to Buddhism. In Bihar, large numbers of Untouchables have become Muslims.

Though it seems alien to Westerners reared on ideas of equality, India's caste system was founded on solid inherent virtues. It provides every individual with a social framework that orders his life and gives him a guild to look after his interests. Yet over the centuries, the system has been corrupted to serve those in power, making Untouchables the outcastes that they still remain. At worst, Untouchables suffer physical violence at the hands of their compatriots, at best the psychological violence of ostracism. Many people, both within and outside India, consider the position of the Scheduled Castes a violation of human dignity.

Life has generally been difficult for Hindu women, too. There are passages from the Vedas that grant women an honorable place alongside men, and in the Vedic age, women were allowed to become priests. Subsequently, however, their roles became much more circumscribed. Like the Shudras and Untouchables, they were cut off from the mainstream of religious activity by being denied access to the Vedic hymns and myths. The Laws of Manu—the canon law of Hinduism, compiled in the second or third century A.D.—enjoin a woman to worship her husband as a god, no matter how basely he behaves. "If a wife obeys her husband, she will, for that reason alone, be exalted in heaven." With the sanction of Hindu tradition, females at all levels of society have been treated for centuries as secondary to the male in all respects.

Discrimination begins at birth. In

THE FUTURE IN THE PALM OF A HAND

Practitioners of the predictive arts enjoy a wide clientele among Indians, who regularly have their stars, their palms, even their shadows read and interpreted. Most public events take place on astrologically auspicious days, and individuals arrange journeys and business deals according to horoscopes. For the mass market, almanacs are produced with daily schedules of propitious times, down to the second, for every activity from eating meat and taking medicine to riding an elephant and committing robbery.

India's most numerous fortunetellers are the palmists, whom many consider more precise than astrologers. While time of birth — vital for an accurate horoscope — may be in error, an expert like the traveling palmist above can reliably read the lines of the hand.

Seated in front of a black iron box that holds the sacred fire, the young bride and groom receive a blessing from their priest. A video camera makes a record of the ceremony, bringing a contemporary note to the flower-bedecked wedding bower.

SPLENDORS OF A WEDDING DAY

An arranged marriage, joining two wealthy Bombay families, displays on a lavish scale the elements essential to all Hindu weddings. On a day chosen by an astrologer, the traditionally dressed couple — the groom in a turban, the bride in a pink or red sari — proceeds through a lengthy ceremony. In the end, they take seven steps, each representing an aspect of marital success, before a fire symbolic of fidelity. Sprinkling holy water, the priest seals the match, and a festive dinner follows.

Hindu families are bound by tradition to provide elaborate weddings, a custom that can lead to crippling debt. Today, some charitable temples offer mass weddings, supplying everything from the astrologer to the feast.

Swathed in a costly sari of embroidered pink silk, the demure bride sits with folded hands that her female relatives have decorated with elaborate designs in henna. The dye will last for weeks, betokening her new status as a wife.

primitive rural areas, cases are still reported from time to time of girl babies being allowed to die by poor families, who would have kept them alive had they been boys. One reason sons are more valued is simply that they are stronger, capable of more heavy work in the fields. Another is that, according to Hindu rite, it is the oldest son who must light the funeral pyre for his dead father. If a man has no sons, another close male relative may perform the duty, but to have no man at all to perform the office would be humiliating. Last but not least, daughters are more of a problem because they will need a dowry when they marry.

Like caste, dowries are forbidden in law—by the Dowry Prohibition Act of 1961—but flourish all the same in India. Some parents cripple themselves financially by providing dowries, while others grow rich on the pickings that come their way by marrying off their sons. The size of the dowry depends on the education and job of the son. A workman may be offered no more than a bicycle or a motor scooter, while an office boy can expect to attract the equivalent of $1,500 to $3,000. A young man in the professions, particularly if he has been to a European or North American university, can command sums in the region of $45,000 or more. Usually the dowry is paid and everyone lives happily ever after, more or less. Sometimes, however, the bridegroom's family regards the dowry as nothing more than a down payment and tries to extract additional sums later on. Occasionally, this begins an appalling sequence of events that in the past few years has become a small epidemic, with historical echoes of *sati.*

"Sati," which literally means "true wife," was common in India until the middle of the 19th century. If a Hindu man died, his widow was sometimes burned alive at the cremation of his corpse. Her acceptance of this fate was seen as the greatest offering of true love. The British thought it a barbarity, as did a great many Indians. It was virtually stamped out in the 19th century, though isolated incidents have been known to take place since. In August 1980, in a Rajasthani village, a 16-year-old girl named Om Kanwar, dressed in the clothes she had lately worn on her wedding day, burned to death at her husband's cremation, while a large crowd stood and watched. The place has been a regional shrine ever since.

The bride burning of recent years has nothing to do with love, misguided or otherwise. It follows from greed, and from the convention that the bride takes up residence in the home of her in-laws after the marriage ceremony. If the in-laws are of a mind to extort more money after the dowry has been paid, the pressure of their demands falls mainly on the bride herself, not on her parents. Some young women have been driven to suicide as a result. Others have obviously been murdered by their in-laws when the pressure has failed to produce more cash.

In either case, the bride has had what has officially been described as an accident in the kitchen, where cooking is generally done on alcohol-burning stoves. She has died as a result of burns. In Delhi, more than 500 young women died in this fashion in 1981 alone. The general public was alerted to the dowry deaths by the investigations of local newspapers. Inquiries in 1982 brought to light the case of the Delhi businessman who had been widowed three times since 1975. Each of his wives died from burns in the kitchen.

Such inhumanity is relatively rare. But even if her new family is welcoming, a bride's lot often looks unenviable to Western eyes. She will be virtually confined to the house and the family plot, never escaping her husband's parents, his brothers and their wives—people who were strangers to her before her marriage. She must learn to submit to two sources of control in all things: her husband and her in-laws. If she wants to go to the doctor or to see her own mother, she will have to seek permission, which may well be refused. She rarely even has a say in how many children she will bear.

The young woman does achieve a form of authority in her own right when she becomes a mother, but even then she will not find life easy if her mother-in-law is still alive. Respect for her husband's family forbids her to fondle her own children in the presence of the older generation, yet if her mother-in-law chooses to make much of her child, she must not protest. Nowadays, a well-educated young woman may find she can dominate a mother-in-law who has had less schooling, but most daughters-in-law are still expected to act submissively. Not surprisingly, the tensions between mothers- and daughters-in-law are a staple theme of Indian films.

For all the difficulties encountered by a young wife, they are slight when compared with the lot of a widow. The abolition of *sati* did not end widows' tribulations, for Hindu tradition forbids the remarriage of widows or even of girls betrothed in infancy. In practice, only high castes enforce the ban—one of the commonest ploys of a caste trying to improve its status is to deny widows the right of remarriage. The widow continues to live with her dead

As the mother and a priest look on, a father confers spiritual adulthood on his son by slipping over the boy's shoulder a sacred thread, three cotton strands woven by a virgin girl. Celebrated with fruit and flower offerings to the gods, the ceremony is a prerequisite for scriptural study and marriage.

husband's family and is treated by them with little regard.

Although so many Hindu practices seem to the disadvantage of women, it is women who uphold the customs and caste rules most rigorously. Hindu women also observe their religious obligations much more faithfully than men. The majority of Indian women accept the workings of society and their role in it with equanimity, or at the very least with resignation.

A fast-growing minority of educated women in the cities, however, is questioning the traditional rules and striving to change them. Feminism in its modern guise arrived in India from the West in the early 1970s. But it was hardly a new idea there: Many of the principles behind it had fueled social reform movements in the 19th century and the nationalist movement of the 20th century; and a most unlikely assortment of people, both British and Indian, devoted themselves to improving the lot of Indian womanhood. They have included Indian atheists and Christian missionaries, British governors general and Mahatma Gandhi.

Their efforts enjoyed a limited success. Calcutta University, for example, allowed women to matriculate in 1877—in England, Oxford and Cambridge began to admit women around the same time—and by the 1920s, words such as "emancipation" had become an accepted part of political rhetoric. Women became activists in the Independence movement. In Bengal, some even became terrorists.

Following Independence, Indian governments translated the rhetoric into legislation that consolidated the previous rudimentary laws, passed by the British, forbidding the practice of *sati* and permitting widows to remarry.

2

At dawn in Rajasthan, an Untouchable sweeps the street — a job relegated to those born outside the four caste groups. Manu, an ancient Hindu lawgiver, wrote of the outcastes, "Their wealth shall be dogs and donkeys, their dress the garments of the dead."

In theory, women drew level with men in terms of position and opportunities in virtually every sphere of Indian life. The Factories Act of 1948 encouraged the provision of nurseries; the Hindu Succession Act of 1956 secured the right of women to inherit property; abortion was legalized in 1971.

Such legislation, unfortunately, did not translate automatically into social change. "The new feminist movement was born with the realization that none of these laws was actually working," says Urvashi Butalia, the cofounder of India's first feminist publishing house. Among other things, she points to the fact that 46 percent of Indian men can read and write, whereas only 25 percent of women in India are literate.

Butalia is a single woman in her mid-thirties who grew up in Delhi in a liberal middle-class household where caste was ignored; her mother is a college lecturer of the Kshatriya *varna,* her father a journalist of mixed Sikh and Hindu descent. Like so many of her coactivists, she first became involved with the movement during a series of demonstrations against dowry deaths in 1978. A feminist magazine, *Manushi,* began publication the following year. Today, there are hundreds of women's groups spread throughout India. "At first we picked on the issues that seemed the easiest to focus public attention on," says Butalia. She lists such topics as dowry deaths and "eve-teasing" (an Indian euphemism for molestation). But very soon it became obvious to her that feminism in India would also have to take account of much more basic issues; the fact, for example, that poor Indian women often have to do the hardest work in the home and yet have the least to eat.

She stresses the qualitative difference between the feminist movements in India and in the West. "We have to take account of health, hunger and general poverty. Men, as well as women, are suppressed and starved in India, and we have to acknowledge the circumstances which force a man to allow his daughter to die rather than his son. Sexual politics of the New York or London kind are a luxury here."

Yet Butalia is the first to admit that the successes of the movement she helped initiate have so far been largely confined to middle-class urban women. Many professions of high visibility—for example, journalism and advertising—have been invaded by women over the past 10 years. Popular movies have also started to feature women as intelligent, rather than mere objects of desire. "I think that at least some Indian women now lead more independent lives," says Butalia. "They have more interesting jobs and they may even have a marginally more equal relationship with their husbands. Some men have been known to cook and look after the children occasionally."

But she suspects that these achievements have stopped at the city limits. "India is a very complex country and it's dangerous to generalize, but I can say from my own contact with poor village women that very little has altered for them. They understand what we're talking about, but persuading them to see the possibility of change is difficult. Our work is only just beginning."

Although there is so much still to do, she takes heart from the fact that three of the most important deities in the Hindu pantheon are women: Kali for power, Lakshmi for prosperity, Saraswati for learning. "I think you could say we can hark back to something which is pretty potent." □

PILGRIMS IN THE CITY OF SALVATION

Photographs by J. Henebry

To Hindus, the ancient city of Varanasi—known in the Mogul and British eras as Benares—is the holiest place on earth. This, they believe, is the spot that the great god Shiva picked as his worldly home after his marriage to the lovely goddess Parvati. The city lies on the bank of the Ganges, a river that, according to Hindu tradition, once flowed through the spheres of heaven.

For centuries, Varanasi has drawn pilgrims from all over India. In the past, they came on foot; today, many people travel by train or bus, but some still walk, for those who joyfully endure the rigors along the way can be sure that any immoral acts they may have committed in this life will be wiped out. Besides millions of ordinary citizens making a once-in-a-lifetime journey, Varanasi attracts ascetics and holy men who have renounced all worldly ties and wait only for their release from human bondage. If they die in Varanasi, their souls go straight to heaven, escaping the persistent cycle of death and rebirth that is the lot of other mortals. But Varanasi confers this benefit even on those who have not lived as holy men: Many come to the city at the eleventh hour to await death and liberation.

The Ganges is the destination for both the living and the dead in Varanasi. Along the three-mile stretch of the city's waterfront, pilgrims congregate at the foot of flights of stone steps—known as ghats—that lead down to the river. There, while washermen flog garments clean, children splash about, astrologers read horoscopes and yogis perform improbable contortions, the pilgrims immerse themselves to wash away their misdeeds. The deceased are cremated near the bank of the Ganges, then their ashes are scattered on its waters, whence their souls will enter the realm of bliss.

A jumble of temples crowds Varanasi's steep riverfront. Most of them are dedicated to Shiva, destroyer of evil and author of good, and the city's streets are lined with lingas: stone shafts that are shrines to the god.

A young man, his high caste signified by the sacred thread he wears over his left shoulder, stands at prayer in the Ganges. Hindus use the repetition of holy words or phrases to induce a meditative state, thereby reaching a higher spiritual plane.

At the foot of one of the ghats, a woman launches an offering of flowers into the river. Hindus worship the Ganges as a mother goddess, giver of nourishment to the countryside and its people.

While priests perform rituals for a fee beneath improvised umbrellas, pilgrims pray and wash in the Ganges. The women immerse themselves fully dressed

and then change their wet garments for dry saris when they emerge.

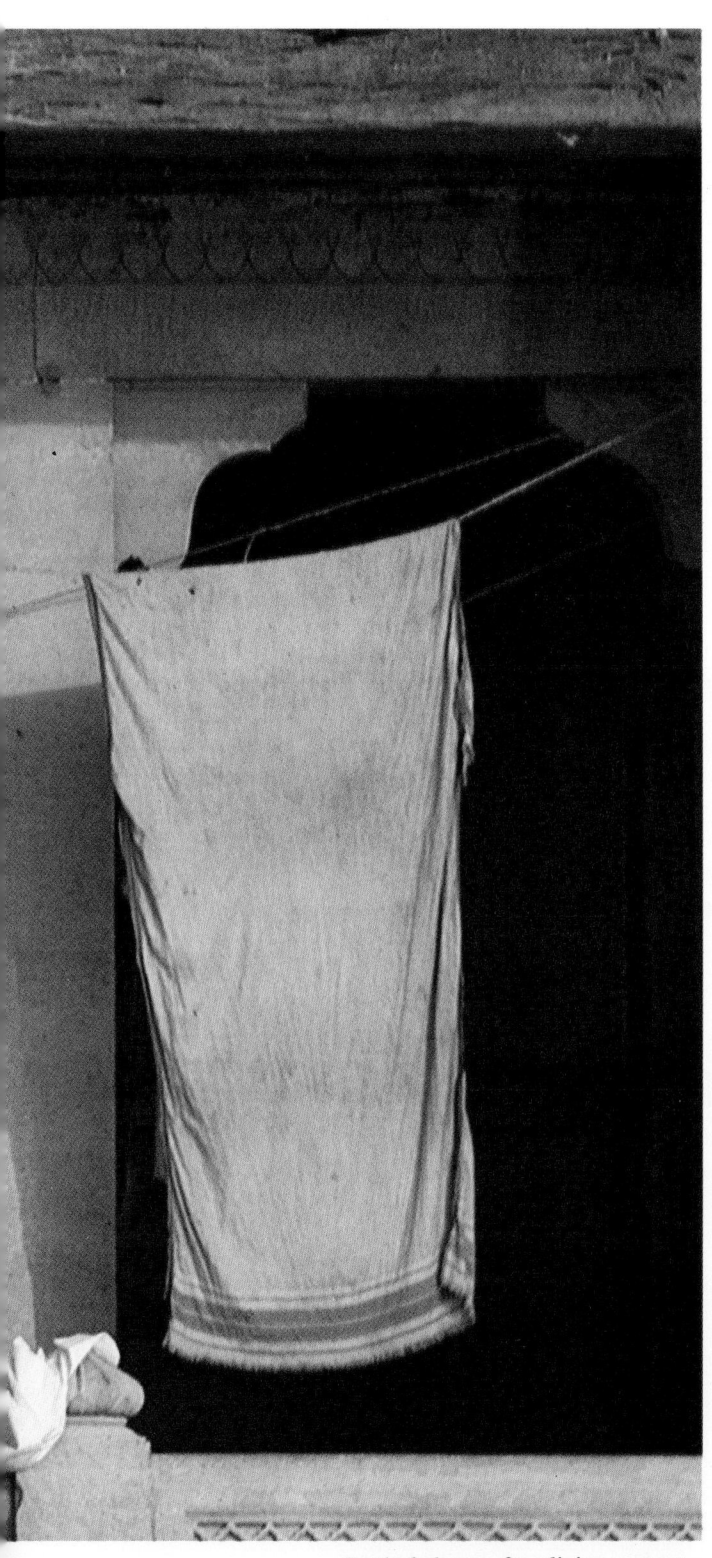

On the balcony of a religious retreat, a worshipper greets the dawn with outstretched arms. The sun is honored in Varanasi as the giver of enlightenment.

Framed by the portico of his lodging, an elderly man studies the scriptures. The horizontal white lines on his brow mark him as a follower of Shiva.

Camped beneath a gaily painted water tower, a pair of wandering holy men prepare for the day. While one paints his forehead with the vertical stripes that signify fidelity to the god Vishnu, the other performs his devotions with the aid of prayer beads.

A family of pilgrims presents gifts of flowers, leaves, rice and sweets to the goddess Shitala, the protector against smallpox, in her temple overlooking the Ganges. With his hand outstretched, the priest sitting among them helps them to conduct the ritual.

With his head shaved according to custom, a man wearing a seamless white garment flings a taper of burning straw onto his father's funeral pyre. All who can afford it are consumed with sandalwood, whose perfumed smoke disguises the stench of burning flesh.

At one of Varanasi's two cremation grounds, attendants prod fires with long poles as flames consume the bodies of the deceased. In most Indian towns, the dead, deemed unclean, are burned outside the city. But in Varanasi, death is auspicious, and the cremation sites are in the center.

In a wall painting from a Buddhist cave temple at Ajanta in Maharashtra, a raja, flanked by his son, discusses a proposal of marriage with his beautiful daughter. The mural dates from the golden age of Indian art — the fifth century, when the Gupta Empire was at its height.

CENTURIES OF FOREIGN RULE

At first sight, the Indian subcontinent is impressively protected from the outside world. To the south there is the ocean; and the formidable northern barrier of the Himalayas is flanked on the west by desert and on the east by nearly impenetrable rain forest. Even so, few nations have enjoyed less isolation than India, and a long succession of foreign overlords has contributed enormously to its complex evolution.

India's earliest civilization, however, was indigenous. Appropriately, its birthplace was the valley of the mighty Indus River, which later gave its name both to India itself and to the subcontinent's dominant religion. Around 4,500 years ago, cities began to rise among the scattered agricultural settlements that had existed from time immemorial on the Indus plain. Directed by the two primary centers of Harappa, southwest of modern Lahore in present-day Pakistan, and Mohenjo-Daro, to the north of modern Hyderabad, an organized society eventually extended its control to an area of almost 400,000 square miles. Its cities, solidly built of stone, were arranged in a grid pattern of streets around a high citadel and a granary. They were equipped with a drainage system far more advanced than anything India was to see until modern times.

From the partitioned layouts of the cities, archeologists conjecture that the Indus Valley civilization may have been a stratified society of priests, merchants and farmers, prefiguring the caste structure of Hinduism, just as the religious statuary unearthed from its ruins foreshadows the gods and goddesses of the Hindu pantheon. Most of our knowledge of the Indus civilization, however, is based merely on educated guesswork: The unique script used by its people has never been deciphered, and there are no other records. Around 1500 B.C., after a continuous existence of 1,000 years, it vanished from the face of the earth. There are signs that for a century or two before its end, the Indus civilization was in decline. Archeologists have noted that the streets no longer followed a careful grid pattern, drainage disappeared, houses diminished in size, and pottery deteriorated in quality. But its extinction was brought about by outside forces. In the middle of the second millennium B.C., India was overwhelmed by the first of many invaders: the Aryans.

The Aryans came from the grasslands of central Asia, probably around the Caspian Sea, and there they lived a nomadic life based on cattle raising. Their sudden, dramatic expansion—still unexplained, but probably provoked by a population explosion—was one of the great migrations in world history. One group swept into Europe; a second fell upon the civilizations of Mesopotamia—"their onslaught was like a hurricane," a contemporary Mesopotamian chronicler wrote. And a third wave descended into India.

3

The details of the Aryan conquest of India are forever lost to us; apart from the fragmentary evidence of archeology, the Aryans' great epic poems are virtually the sole source for the history of the next millennium. These works—among them the Ramayana and the Mahabharata—are also the world's most remarkable example of an oral tradition, for they were not committed to writing until around 400 B.C. or even later. Their verses present a picture of internecine struggles and conquest, chivalry and guile. Although the narrative takes mythological form, and gods participate in the action alongside mortals, scholars have deduced the broad outlines of early Indian history by reading between the lines.

As Aryan rule spread through northern India and as far south as the Deccan—the vast plateau of central India—there emerged a patchwork of small kingdoms, sharing a common culture but prone to warring among themselves. The great epics exalted combat, but they also exalted the priesthood. Brahmins, or priests, were subordinate to warriors in Aryan society, but the people's anxiety to placate the gods in the correct manner elevated the Brahmins to an immensely influential position. As time passed and the Aryan conquerors swallowed up more and more of the subcontinent's indigenous cultures, their gods and their world views, the religion of the Aryan people evolved, by accretion, into the complexity of Hinduism and the caste system. By around 200 A.D., the whole edifice was firmly in place.

The lofty status accorded to Brahmins had two interesting effects. First, it attached a high value to religious thinking and philosophical concepts. Almost from the beginning of Indian history, the guru—the teacher, usually poor, often wandering and invariably engrossed in the great concepts of eternity—has been accorded reverence. Second, the Brahmin domination of orthodox religion gave an incentive to the lower castes to seek assurance of their own worth elsewhere. In the sixth century B.C., the two factors combined to produce India's second great religion: Buddhism, founded in northern India by Siddartha Gautama, the Buddha or the "awakened one."

Essentially, Buddhism offered its adherents a path to enlightenment that was open to all, regardless of caste: Its appeal was immediate. The religion's success proved most enduring outside its Indian homeland; it transformed Tibet, China and Japan, and some people consider it to be India's greatest contribution to civilization. In its birthplace, however, it has always been the religion of a minority.

In the absence of written records, India's early history remains shadowy, but in 326 B.C., Alexander the Great of Macedon mounted an expedition to the subcontinent and dispelled some of the mystery. Numerous memoir writers in Alexander's army gave Westerners a kind of "You Are There" picture of Indian society in the fourth century B.C. They described warring kings, in shifting arrangements of tribute and alliance, who fought with vast armies that included terrifying armored elephants; strange social customs, such as *sati*—the burning alive of a widow upon her husband's funeral pyre; and the Hindu gurus, whom they dubbed gymnosophists, which literally means "naked philosophers." The gurus made a deep impression on the Greeks, and at least one of them accompanied Alexander on his return march.

Indian chronicles, however, make no reference to Alexander's brief appearance. But Alexander may have served as an instructive example to at least one important Indian: Chandragupta Maurya, who in the years following the Greek withdrawal in 325 B.C. established an empire that ran from the mountainous northwest to the Bay of Bengal in the east. Chandragupta and his successors built a highly organized state whose influence eventually extended as far south as Mysore.

The great Mauryan Empire, based at Patna beside the Ganges, reached its peak under the extraordinary Emperor Ashoka, around 250 B.C. Ashoka, the grandson of Chandragupta, was perhaps the most idealistic of all India's rulers. Early in his career, he had snuffed out the independence of the last surviving Bengali kingdom of Kalinga with the method common at the time: slaughter. But far from glorying in his conquest, he was stricken by remorse. He adopted Buddhism and promulgated laws—based on the assumption of the sanctity of life—that were carved in rock and on stone columns throughout his empire. One of them—the lion column of Sarnath—became the emblem of the Republic of India more than 2,000 years later. But neither Ashoka's empire nor his laws long survived his death in 232 B.C.; within a few generations, even his name was forgotten, and his inscriptions were not deciphered until 1837. Waves of foreign invaders once more beleaguered northern India.

After the Maurya, no rulers of India were to control so much of the subcontinent for more than two millennia to come; apart from their brief taste of Mauryan authority, the Deccan and the south would go their own way. There, myriad kingdoms rose, endured a few hundred years and then declined. Meanwhile, grander dramas were being played out in the north.

Almost 600 years after the end of the Mauryan Empire, another great dynasty established itself in northern India. Founded in the fourth century A.D., the empire of the Gupta line of kings embraced the whole breadth of the subcontinent, from Punjab to Bengal. Although the Gupta Empire never reached as far south as in the days of Ashoka, it made up for its more modest dimensions by presiding over a great flowering of Indian culture. Art, philosophy and science—particularly mathematics, where Indian scholars were exploring the concept of zero—all reached new heights. But the Gupta Empire lasted little more than 200 years. In the fifth century, India fell to barbarian hordes from central Asia and entered a period as turbulent as Europe's concurrent Dark Ages.

In the early seventh century, the adventurer-emperor Harshavardhana reunified most of the old Gupta territory, but his achievement did not outlive him. In any case, a new world force was about to make its presence felt. This time, it came not from central Asia but from the Middle East, and it was to change India permanently.

The Prophet Muhammad died in 632; and not long after he died, the Prophet's new religion of Islam burst from its Arabian birthplace in a torrent. It swept westward around the Mediterranean, southward into Africa and east through Persia into central Asia and what is now Afghanistan. In 712, the Arab faithful conquered the western Indian province of Sind, where Islam soon established roots: The new religion made converts not only by the persuasive arguments of fire and the sword but also by its powerful appeal to low-caste and outcaste Hindus.

A fifth-century Buddha sculpted in sandstone sits in cross-legged meditation, his head framed by an ornate halo. The figures at the foot of the pedestal represent the disciples who made up the audience for his first sermon.

Nevertheless, Islamic power was, for a time, restricted to the Indus Valley. The various Hindu states, though without the might to throw the invaders back, were strong enough to maintain their frontiers, thanks primarily to the Rajput warriors who gave their name to modern-day Rajasthan.

The Rajputs were not so much a race as a network of more-or-less related warlike clans ruled by a kind of military aristocracy. Almost certainly descendants of barbarian invaders, they had been adroitly assimilated into the caste system at a high level and provided India with a defensive belt of vigorously independent border lords, known for their chivalry as well as for their dangerously touchy pride. With the Rajputs guarding the gate, India was relatively well-protected against invasion from the west.

The next wave of Muslim conquerors, however, came from the north in the early 11th century. To begin with, the object was plunder, not rule: The voracious Sultan of Ghazni in Afghanistan saw no reason why he and his warriors should not relieve the infidel Hindus of their wealth, and they raided southward as far as the coastal city of Somnath. For 30 years, the sultan's bloodthirsty excursions were almost an annual event; the inability of ponderous, elephant-equipped Hindu armies to come to grips with the speedy northern horsemen did not bode well.

Nevertheless, raiding was one thing and conquest another. Not until the late 12th century, while Hindu energies were thoroughly committed to internal quarrels, did the Afghans attempt any serious invasions, under Muhammad Ghuri. In the beginning, they were repulsed by fragile Rajput coalitions, but when Muhammad Ghuri returned in 1192, Rajput unity had dissolved, and he was able to crush his opponents in pitched battle. The result was the so-called Delhi Sultanate, which held sway over northern India until the 16th century.

The sultanate spent most of its first 200 years expanding, until its rule—for the first time since the long-forgotten Emperor Ashoka—extended far to the south. But it proved almost impossible to administer so vast a domain from Delhi, and an attempt in the 14th century to solve the problem by moving the capital southward, to Devagiri in the Deccan, was successful only in making the northern provinces as unmanageable as the southern ones had been.

عمل منوهر

VIGNETTES OF COURT LIFE IN THE MOGUL ERA

Under the Mogul emperors, the subcontinent achieved extraordinary heights of beauty and refinement in the art of miniature painting. The art form fused the indigenous genius for vivid color with Persian technical virtuosity and delight in decoration.

The flowering of Mogul art began in the mid-16th century under Akbar, an enthusiastic and discriminating patron. Employing Persian immigrants to supervise Indian artists in his court atelier, he commissioned illustrations from Persian stories and Hindu epics. Akbar's successors demanded a new subject range from painters — chiefly portraits and palace scenes. The emperors collected European paintings and prints, and Mogul art came to incorporate Western elements such as perspective and chiaroscuro.

Like their masters, the emperors' Hindu vassals installed artists at their courts. Paintings executed for the Rajput princes of Rajasthan and the Himalayan foothills were strongly influenced by the imperial style. But while Mogul art deteriorated with the emperors' decline in the 18th century, the Rajput school produced lively works for another hundred years.

In a flower-bordered miniature *(far left)*, Mogul Emperor Shah Jahan rides through a mountainous stretch of his realm. Courtiers escort him, and his son rides behind. In 1610, when this work was first completed by court artist Manohar, the emperor depicted was Shah Jahan's father, Jahangir. After Shah Jahan's succession in 1627, another artist changed the face to portray the new ruler. The painting at left was executed in the 18th century at one of the Rajput courts in the Himalayan foothills. In it, Raja Raj Singh of Chamba and his favorite concubine smoke hookahs, which are held by two of their four attendants.

3

A 19th-century English print of the Taj Mahal captures the monument's graceful symmetry. The marble Taj was constructed at Agra by the Mogul emperor Shah Jahan between 1632 and 1653 as a mausoleum for his beloved favorite wife, Mumtaz-i-Mahal.

By the 1350s, the whole imperial colossus was beginning to come apart at the seams. In 1398, it received a death blow from an invasion by Tamerlane, the great conqueror of central Asia. Tamerlane's incursion was brief, but it shattered India's central authority, laying waste to Punjab and leaving the Delhi Sultanate clinging to a small area around its pillaged capital.

In time, the sultanate recovered some of its earlier power, but it never again approached all-India dominion. Its rule, however, had lasting effects. It brought about an intermingling of Muslim and Hindu peoples and ideas, mostly as a result of the policy of religious tolerance that circumstances forced upon it. It also brought about the use of Persian as the official language in place of the ancient Sanskrit. Now that the language of power was foreign to native ears, the eclipse of Sanskrit led to the gradual elevation in status of many of India's previously overshadowed regional tongues.

By the early 16th century, the sultanate's power was largely a memory, and India was once more a collection of suspicious and quarrelsome states. The stage was set for the arrival of yet another outside invader. This time, however, there was to be not one but two new conquering forces. One was to descend through the well-trodden passes from Afghanistan; the other would come from half a world away.

The Europeans were first to arrive on the scene. A Portuguese expedition reached India in 1498, blazing a sea route eastward, which would give Portugal access to the lucrative trade in exotic oriental goods, especially spices. The Portuguese were not interested in empire building: They saw no profit in it. Nevertheless, in order to protect their mercantile interests, they needed to have secure bases, and by the 1520s, they were in control of Goa and a few other enclaves.

While the Portuguese were consolidating their grip upon the spice trade, great events were happening in the north. Babur, Muslim King of Kabul in Afghanistan and—he claimed—a direct descendant of Tamerlane, had been trying to reclaim his ancestral dominions in central Asia for years. But the tough nomads proved to be too difficult to subdue, and Babur decided to try his luck instead in northern India. After two exploratory raids, he launched his invasion late in 1525.

It was a stupendous venture. Babur had only 9,000 men, whom he himself admitted to be "in great tremor and alarm" against the immensity of India. But Babur was an inspired leader, and besides, his tiny army was lavishly equipped with artillery that he had acquired through his association with the Ottoman Turks. His enemies knew nothing of the new weaponry. In a daylong battle in 1526, he routed the vast but ill-coordinated hordes of Ibrahim, last of the Delhi sultans.

The following year, despite another failure of nerve on the part of his own troops, Babur's brilliant generalship routed an even larger host put together by the Rajputs. Somewhat to his own surprise, he found himself master of northern India and the founder of the Mogul Empire.

But Babur's son and successor, Homayun, had none of his father's qualities, and by the time he died, he retained only a precarious toehold on India. However, Homayun's son Akbar was Babur reincarnated. To begin with, he was lucky. Only 13 years old on his accession, he was served loyally by a guardian-regent, who won for him his first critical battle against a usurper tempted by the emperor's extreme youth. (The young Akbar himself decapitated the captured enemy leader.) When he came of age, he ruled his empire with a vigorous combination of wisdom and ruthlessness. Akbar was wise in his policy of attempting to reconcile his Muslim and Hindu subjects, admitting the latter into his increasingly well-organized administration and abolishing discriminatory taxation. Indeed, to cement the bonds of loyalty, he cheerfully married a whole succession of Hindu princesses.

Akbar reserved his ruthlessness for his enemies, real or potential. Thus more than one possible pretender was the victim of a precautionary murder. And in 1568, Akbar destroyed the remnants of the Rajputs' independence at the bloody siege of Chitor, capital of their leading clans.

When the arch-Mogul died in 1605, he passed on a glittering inheritance. Thanks to his marriage policy, his son Jahangir was half-Indian; thenceforth, the Moguls were not an alien power. And although not one of Akbar's successors was his equal, the foundations he had laid ensured the empire's steady expansion—for a time.

By the middle of the 17th century, things had begun to go wrong. Under the Emperor Aurangzeb, Muslim fanaticism began to replace political wisdom. One result was rebellion and civil war, mainly with the Maratha people of the western seaboard. Religious persecution also helped forge the Sikhs, originally a reformist Hindu sect, into the beginnings of a warlike community. Aurangzeb won the wars he had provoked, but at a terrible cost. Soon after

his death, the empire began to disintegrate: Infighting and palace coups were rife. Meanwhile, its distant provinces lapsed into independence, declared or otherwise. By the 1750s, nothing had yet evolved in India that was strong enough to replace the Moguls. It was a vacuum that proved fatal to Indian independence.

In the south, the Portuguese had not enjoyed their trading monopoly for long. In 1600, Queen Elizabeth I of England granted a charter to the merchant-adventurers of the East India Company; two years later, the Dutch created their own company. The object of each was not so much India as the spice islands of Java and the Moluccas, but both sought and obtained bases on the Indian coast, as trading posts and way stations for more lucrative ventures farther east. By the early 17th century, the two increasingly powerful European nations were becoming more than a match for Portugal, which suffered defeats at sea and was barely able to hang on to Goa.

The Dutch very quickly succeeded in dominating Java and its seas. Rather than wasting their capital in a risky effort to oust their rivals, the directors of the English company decided to concentrate on trade with India itself. By 1647, they had established 23 trading posts, most of them on the coast and many of them in the far south, where the writ of the Mogul Empire did not run. The French soon joined the British; they arrived in 1674, establishing a trading post at Pondicherry. And at first, it seemed that there was trade enough for everyone.

By the 1740s, though, Anglo-French rivalry had intensified. Moreover, the Mogul Empire was dying on its feet, and the increasing independence of its former subject princes gave the English and the French great scope for diplo-

3

matic maneuvering at each other's expense. When war broke out between them in Europe in 1744, it was inevitable that they would try to eliminate each other from India.

The war between the British and the French in India lasted, in effect, for almost 20 years and ended in complete victory for the British. The rewards were far greater than either of the combatants had imagined when the fighting started. For during the Anglo-French war, the Mogul Empire at last collapsed. An Afghan army descended on Delhi in 1757 and devastated it. The Marathas, who were hoping to take the Mogul throne for themselves, met the Afghans in pitched battle in 1761; but it was the Marathas who were annihilated. Then, homesick and satisfied with the loot they had already gathered, the Afghans returned to their hills. India was there for the taking; and the British took it.

In 1757, an aggressive commander of the British forces, a 32-year-old former clerk named Robert Clive, won the battle of Plassey, 125 miles north of Calcutta. This victory allowed him to install the ruler of his choice in the vast province of Bengal. Bengal was the first of many new dominions to come directly or indirectly under the control of the East India Company, much to the dismay of its directors in London. They were interested in trade, not empire, and the exploits of young military adventurers such as Clive were costing a fortune. Besides, tales abounded of outrageous mismanagement, by which company employees were enriching themselves in an extravagant manner. The whole business was giving both the company and Britain itself a bad name.

The company sent out a new governor for Bengal, Warren Hastings, with

A painting from a 1646 Portuguese book shows the first English trading post in India under attack by Portuguese rivals. Established in 1612 on a spur of land adjoining the port of Surat, the settlement was the site of many such skirmishes before the British ousted other Europeans from India.

instructions to end abuses, and for the first time, the British government took a hand, passing an act of Parliament designed to control the company's activities. There was to be no more empire building: "The dominion of all India," declared Hastings, promoted by Parliament in 1774 to the new dignity of governor general of Bengal, "is what I never wish to see." Nevertheless, an imperial edifice began to emerge. In 1784, the British Parliament passed another act relating to India. This one imposed a Board of Control, consisting of six government ministers, over the directors of the East India Company. The company still ran its territories and its business in India, but the board had the power of veto on any matter that touched politics.

Conscious of the inherent weakness of their small numbers, India's new ruling elite were at first reluctant to impose much in the way of change upon their subjects. By the 1820s, though, progressive opinion in Britain stressed the nation's responsibility for its subject peoples. Reforms were instituted. *Sati* was abolished in 1829, thanks primarily to the campaigns of Ram Mohan Roy, the brilliant Hindu reformer later known as the "father of modern India." In the 1830s, the governor general stamped out the horrifying practice of *thuggee*—the ritual murder of travelers by gangs that were devoted to the bloodthirsty goddess Kali.

An 1833 act ended the East India Company's trading function, although the British government was anxious to keep its imperial responsibilities at arm's length, and the company maintained its role as a ruling agency. Persian, the legal language of the Moguls, was replaced by English, and under the guidance of Thomas Macaulay—who

A CHRONOLOGY OF KEY EVENTS

c. 2500-1500 B.C. Mohenjo-Daro, Harrapa and other cities flourish in the Indus Valley. Sophisticated urban developments, they produce masterly sculptures in bronze *(below)* and stone.

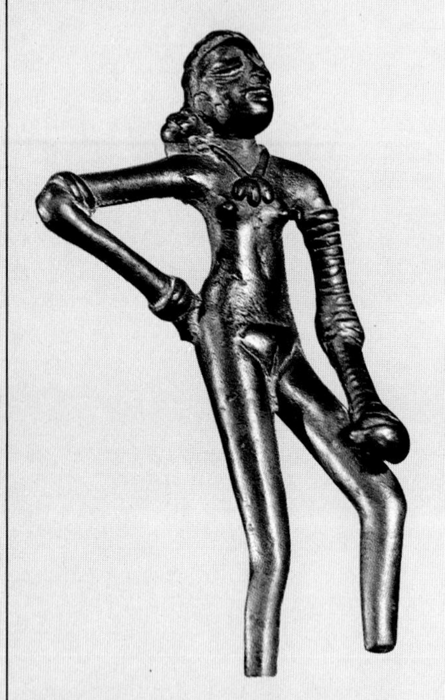

c. 1500 B.C. Light-skinned Aryan invaders from the Caspian Sea area begin to settle northern India, dominating the dark-skinned inhabitants.

c. 1500-1200 B.C. The Vedas, Hindu scriptures, are composed.

c. 563 B.C. Siddhartha Gautama, the Buddha, is born in northeast India.

326 B.C. Alexander the Great of Macedon mounts a campaign in India.

324-185 B.C. The Mauryan emperors rule northern and central India. The greatest Mauryan, Ashoka, brings a unity to India never again equaled until the British raj. His edicts are inscribed on the pillars topped with animal carvings *(right)* that are erected throughout his domain.

320-499 Most of northern India is united under the Gupta dynasty. It is a golden age of literature, art and science: The Hindu temple emerges as India's classic architectural form, and the decimal system is devised.

500-1300 A number of rival powers control southern and central India, among them the Cholas, Pandyas, Cheras, Chalukyas and Pallavas.

712 Muslim incursions into India begin with the conquest of Sind, in the northwest, by Arabs.

997-1027 Afghan raiders repeatedly attack northern India.

1206 The Afghan Qutb-ud-din becomes the first sultan of Delhi, following conquest of the Gangetic plain. The Delhi Sultanate will dominate northern India for 200 years.

1398 Moguls from central Asia, led by Timur (Tamerlane), mount a devastating raid on Delhi.

c. 1490 Guru Nanak founds the Sikh religion in order to reconcile Hinduism with Islam.

1498 The Portuguese navigator Vasco da Gama reaches southern India. With the capture of Goa in 1510, the Portuguese open a century-long monopoly of European trade with India.

1526 King Babur, a Muslim, defeats the sultan of Delhi and establishes Mogul rule in northern India.

1556-1605 Akbar *(above)*, the third Mogul emperor, extends his territory to the Arabian Sea and the Bay of Bengal. He creates a central administration manned by both imported Muslims and native Hindus. Akbar's policy of tolerance fosters a new golden age of Indian culture, this time influenced by Persian motifs.

1600 Elizabeth I of England grants a charter to the East India Company, which proceeds to establish trading posts in Surat (1612), Madras (1640), Bombay (1668) and Calcutta (1690).

1632-1653 Shah Jahan, the fifth Mogul emperor, builds the Taj Mahal in memory of his dead wife Mumtaz.

1674 A French trading post is set up at Pondicherry, south of Madras.

1680 Shivaji Bhonsle, a Hindu warrior-hero, dies after a lifetime of war with the Moguls. The Maratha kingdom that he founded in western India is a dominant power.

1707 Aurangzeb, sixth and last of the great Mogul emperors, dies. Though he has extended his boundaries, his Muslim zealotry has divided and fatally weakened his empire.

1751 Robert Clive, a young British clerk-turned-soldier, leads 210 men to victory over a French force at Arcot. The battle chokes French political ambitions in India.

1756 The nawab of Bengal, theoretically beholden to the Mogul emperors, attacks and occupies Calcutta.

1757 Clive retakes Calcutta and defeats the nawab at the Battle of Plassey, giving the British effective control of Bihar, Orissa and Bengal.

1758 The Maratha kingdom reaches its greatest extent.

1761 Afghan leader Ahmad Shah Abdali defeats the Marathas at Panipat, ending their ambitions in northern India and creating a power vacuum into which the British will step.

1774 Warren Hastings, Bengal's first governor general, lays the foundation of British civil administration.

1813-1818 The East India Company acquires control of the Maratha territory and is acknowledged as suzerain in Rajasthan *(above)*, thus becoming undisputed master of India.

1818-1849 With the annexation of Assam, Sind, Kashmir and Punjab, the East India Company brings all India under its control.

1853 The first Indian railroad opens, to speed cotton to Bombay for shipping to the mills in England.

1857 The Indian Mutiny begins among native soldiers and spreads to others disaffected with British rule. It is crushed after 14 bitter months.

1858 The government of India is transferred from the East India Company to the British Crown.

1877 Queen Victoria is proclaimed Empress of India.

1885 The Indian National Congress holds its inaugural meeting.

1912 India's capital is moved from Calcutta to Delhi.

1913 The Bengali poet Rabindranath Tagore becomes the first nonwhite to win a Nobel Prize.

1914 Gujarati-born Mohandas Gandhi returns to India after living for 21 years in South Africa.

1919 After political disturbances, British troops fire into a large crowd of unarmed Indians in Amritsar, killing nearly 400.

1920 Gandhi becomes head of Congress and launches a campaign for social and political equality, using the weapon of passive noncooperation.

1935 The Government of India Act enfranchises one sixth of the population and makes the provinces autonomous from central government.

1942 As Japanese forces sweep through Burma and threaten India, Gandhi and Congress launch an anti-British "Quit India" movement.

1947 After negotiating with Gandhi and other Indian leaders, Viceroy Louis Mountbatten *(left, below)* grants India independence as a dominion within the British Commonwealth. Jawaharlal Nehru is the first prime minister. Pakistan becomes a separate Muslim state. Hundreds of thousands are massacred in civil strife.

1948 Gandhi is assassinated by a Hindu extremist.

1950 India becomes a federal republic.

1954 Nehru defines India's foreign policy as nonalignment with the superpowers and peaceful coexistence with its neighbors.

1966 Indira Gandhi, Nehru's daughter, becomes prime minister.

1971 A war between Pakistan and India over the latter's support for autonomists in Pakistan's eastern province ends in Indian victory. East Pakistan becomes Bangladesh.

1975-1977 After economic strains and political tensions, Indira Gandhi suspends democracy for 19 months.

1984 After repressing Sikh terrorism in Punjab, Indira Gandhi is assassinated by her Sikh bodyguard. She is succeeded as prime minister by her son, Rajiv Gandhi *(above)*.

THE STORY OF CHINTZ

European and Asian influences merge in a flowering tree on an 18th-century chintz.

Patterned cotton fabric called chintz — plural of the Hindi *chint,* or "spotted cloth' — was among the most sensational imports from India to Europe in the late 17th century. Because Indian dyeing techniques were more advanced than those of Europe, the colors in chintz were extremely bright and durable. The early designs, however, were unpopular with Europeans. So, to improve sales, importers sent Indian chintz-makers sample patterns that were more to French, Dutch or English taste. The Indians' unique interpretation of them appeared wondrously exotic to Europeans.

later became known as a historian—an English-based education system was created, although only a very small minority benefitted from it.

Meanwhile, annexations continued. In the 1840s, Sind was absorbed, and two wars ended Sikh independence. But Britain's conquest of India was haphazard. Large numbers of India's many hereditary rulers put up no resistance to the foreigners. Those posing no threat were allowed to remain on their thrones, and they ran their internal affairs unimpeded.

Many of these rajas and maharajas had no objection to the imperial presence in India; moreover, even those parts of India directly under British rule seemed remarkably docile. The British began to feel they could do no wrong. The acquiescence of the Indians was taken for granted and was used to legitimize British rule: After all, was not the army that enforced it overwhelmingly Indian?

The British were soon to receive a shock. Earlier in the century, a farsighted governor general had warned that the Indian-manned army was "a delicate and dangerous machine, which a little mismanagement may easily turn against us." In 1857, the prediction came true. Discontent, inspired by the relentless annexations and the tradition-breaking reforms, had festered in the army's ranks for some time. Then rumors began to spread that new cartridges issued to the troops were greased with a mixture of cow and pig fat. Since it was army practice to open the cartridges by biting off a twist of paper at one end, both Hindus and Muslims were being asked to violate religious taboos. British insensitivity to this offense lighted the fuse of rebellion: Throughout northern India, army units mutinied, killed their British officers—and often their families. It had been exactly 100 years since Plassey, thoughtful Indians observed. British rule had lasted long enough.

The British called it the Indian Mutiny; later the Indians were to name it the Great War of Independence. The British description is nearer the truth, for most of India remained loyal. The rebellion was confined to the Ganges plain between Calcutta and Delhi; troops in the south and west continued to serve the British. Decisively, the recently conquered Sikhs were quiet. Among the staunchest supporters of the British were the native princes who had been left in nominal control of large parts of the country.

But the uprising was not quite the simple affair of mutinous troops that the British wanted to believe. In Delhi, which quickly fell to the rebels, the last descendant of the Mogul dynasty, the 82-year-old Bahadur Shah, was proclaimed emperor, and for a time, it seemed that he might gain the approval of all Indians.

In the event, the issue was not decided by appeals to hearts and minds, but by bayonets. Most of the fighting was done by soldiers who were *in situ* at the time of the uprising, including large contingents of loyal Indian troops. Not until a late stage did reinforcements from England arrive in any numbers. A four-month siege broke the rebels' hold on Delhi. Meanwhile, the British overwhelmed Kanpur, also a rebel stronghold. In November 1857, Lucknow, another hotbed of revolt, fell to British forces. By January 1859, the last of the rebel armies had been hunted down. Everywhere, the British exacted bloody retribution for the massacres that had begun the uprising.

The rebellion was the great watershed in the history of British India. Afterward, there was never any doubt that British rule was ultimately based not on moral superiority but on armed force, ruthlessly wielded. The mutiny's most immediate consequence was a military reorganization, expressly designed to keep the proportion of European troops at a safely high level. The mutiny also marked the end of what might be termed the adventurers' empire, with its swashbuckling opportunism, and its replacement by the Victorian empire, an altogether more straitlaced creation. For in 1858, the old East India Company was abolished, and the British government assumed formal responsibility for the subcontinent. The governor general found himself elevated to the exalted post of viceroy. The pattern of administration that was to shape India until Independence—and in some ways long afterward—was now established.

The key institution was the Indian Civil Service (ICS), an elite body of only 1,000 highly trained officers, on whom awesome powers were bestowed: It was by no means unusual for a fairly junior ICS man to be responsible for a province of more than a million people. Entry to the august service was by competitive examination and, in theory, was open to Indians. But enrollment involved making a trip to Britain, which was not only costly but prohibited by the religion of high-caste Hindus, since it took them outside the sacred circle of Hinduism and exposed them to all manner of defilement. Inevitably, the service remained overwhelmingly British.

The ICS, aloof and patrician, served, in many ways, as a model for the rest of the British community. The events of 1857, and the mutual fears and mistrust they inspired, had widened the gap between the conquerors and the conquered. The opening of the Suez Canal in 1869, cutting travel time between India and Britain to one month, segregated the two cultures even more. Now that regular home leave had become practical, British women "came out" to India in far greater numbers than before and the British became a self-contained enclave.

British rule brought India many of the fruits of 19th-century progress. Ir-

A life-size wooden tiger, a toy of the 18th-century Indian despot Tipu Sultan, attacks a fallen European to the accompaniment of mechanical growls and screams. Tipu ruled the southern state of Mysore and engaged in numerous wars against the British.

3

rigation projects brought vast areas of land under cultivation; and the 1860s saw a spate of railway building. The railroads were a mixed blessing to Indians, however, for the government guaranteed stockholders in Britain a return—usually 5 percent—whether or not the railways made a profit. Since profits were rare, the Indian government had to meet its obligations to shareholders with revenues from the population at large. The unfairness of this arrangement led to the first economic arguments for self-rule.

As the British saw it, the greatest benefit they were bringing to India was peace. Freed from the plague of civil war, India was developing at a rate exceeded in Asia only by Japan. Calcutta, the raj's capital, was the home of Asia's first European-style middle class, and Bombay was not far behind. The rising middle class provided not only traders and professionals but also industrialists. Great new textile industries were made possible by the arrival of rail transportation, and made profitable by India's entry, as part of the British Empire, into the world economy. Although the jute mills of Bengal were initiated and controlled by Europeans, Bombay's cotton industry was financed, owned and managed almost entirely by Indians. Later, in the early 20th century, steel followed the same pattern as cotton.

The British legal and administrative network did not cover all India. One third of its territory remained under the control of those Indian princes who had been loyal during the Great War of Independence. Their reward was hereditary autonomy that endured as long as the British raj. There were more than 500 such states in India, ranging in size from the 82,313 square miles of Hyderabad, under its fabulously rich Nizam, to impoverished little city-states barely a morning's walk across. Their independence was limited, of course: There was no doubt who was paramount on the subcontinent, and maharajas great and lowly had to put up with the constant presence of a viceroy-appointed British Resident at their courts. The penalty for any anti-British conspiracy was instant removal, by force if necessary, and the grosser forms of misgovernment were also punished by removal from power.

Within these limits, though, India's princely states were left much to their own devices. Many of them pursued admirably progressive policies. Mysore, for instance, eventually developed its own democratic institutions, as well as a modern educational system and the first hydroelectric plant to be built in India. Other rulers devoted themselves less to public progress than private vices, or distinguished themselves by extravagantly free-spending tours of Europe and America, delighting Western newspaper readers at the expense of their impoverished subjects.

British officialdom had always shown a great deal of outward respect for traditional India and its ruling class. As the 19th century advanced, and a series of gentle reforms appointed a few Indians to the machinery of government, it was to aristocratic Indians of the old order that the British turned. However, the future of India did not lie with the people whom the British had effectively supplanted, but with the new, European-educated classes that British rule had created.

The British were remarkably slow to realize that their own policies had brought into being the forces that

An oil painting depicts red-coated British forces engaging mutineers from the Indian Army outside Lucknow in March 1858. The rebels had taken the city in June of the previous year, just after the beginning of the Great War of Independence.

3

would, in time, bring an end to the raj. So, when the Indian National Congress was founded in 1885 (with the aid of a group of retired British ICS officers), the government of India welcomed it cautiously as a forum that might promote better relations between governors and governed. Congress' initial, modest aims were to represent the interests of Western-educated Indians and to present the case for more Indian involvement in government decisions. But it grew into a powerful nationalist movement, which eventually became a post-Independence governing party.

Although barely 1 percent of the population could read and write English, the British-educated minority was an active one. Before long, Congress pressure had secured a series of political reforms. The first, in 1892, was an Indian Councils Act that allowed a form of election to various legislative councils whose membership had hitherto been nominated by the viceroy. The Councils Act was followed in 1909 by the so-called Morley-Minto Reforms, which permitted a measure of local self-government. The British may have hoped that such steps would appease the increasingly nationalistic middle-class community; predictably, however, the reforms merely increased Indian expectations.

In the early 20th century, the nationalist movement became seriously complicated by religious issues. Congress was still open to all Indians; but India's Muslim community had been much slower than the Hindu majority to develop the outward-looking middle class from which Congress members were recruited. As a result, Congress was disproportionately Hindu. The imbalance became important around the turn of the century, with the appearance of an extremist wing that was not only violently nationalist but violently Hindu. Muslims became deeply suspicious that *swaraj* ("home rule," the new slogan of a growing number of Congressmembers) meant Hindu rule.

Matters came to a head in 1905, when the viceroy, Lord Curzon, effected the partition of the vast, populous province of Bengal, splicing the Hindu west from the Muslim east. For Curzon, it may have been simply a question of administrative efficiency, but it looked very much like a policy of divide and conquer. Hindu extremists saw the plan as a threat to "Mother India" and launched a campaign of demonstrations that was soon transformed by British repression into one of riots, bombings and assassinations. It was the worst outbreak of violence since the mutiny 50 years before, and it alarmed Indian Muslims. In 1906, they formed the All-India Muslim League, the first sign that the road to independence might also be the road to separation.

The turmoil of 1905 was soon contained, and in the years before World War I, India seemed peaceful enough. Although the first few steps toward self-rule had been taken, the road to independence still had no end in sight. As if to prove it, the British moved their capital from Calcutta to New Delhi, which they had lavishly built in high imperial style beside the old Mogul city.

The war changed everything. India remained loyal to Britain, and 600,000 Indians fought for the Allies overseas. But afterward, at the peace conference in Versailles, Indians paid careful attention to high-sounding rhetoric about the right to self-determination. India's wartime services were rewarded by the British with a major reform permitting directly elected provincial leg-

Nationalist leader Mahatma Gandhi wears a homespun dhoti for an interview with the press in August 1934, at the start of one of many fasts he undertook to apply moral pressure on the British or his countrymen. Gandhi adopted the peasant garment in 1921 to symbolize his pride in his own culture.

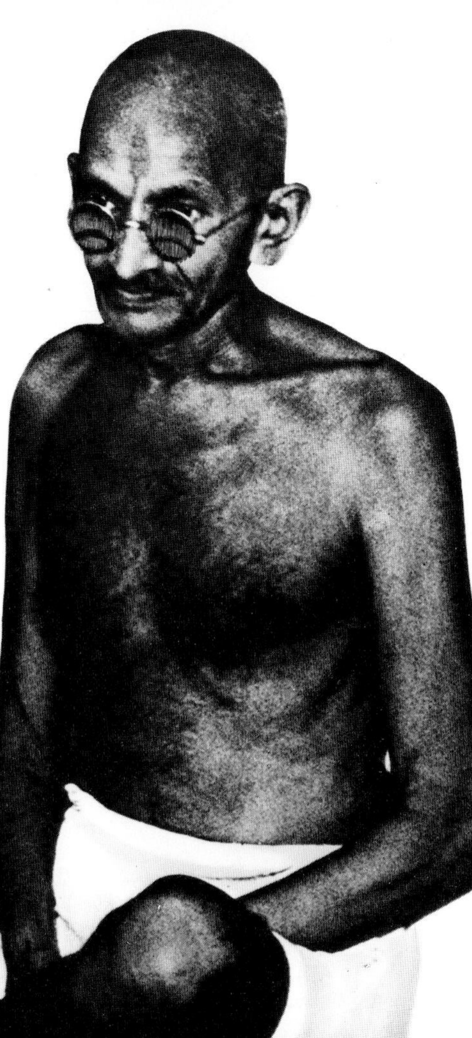

islatures. As in 1909, the gesture was not enough to satisfy the nationalists.

In 1919, there was widespread rioting in Punjab; British troops sent to quell the worst outbreak, in the city of Amritsar, killed almost 400 unarmed people in a few minutes' firing in the public garden known as Jallianwalla Bagh. For years to come, the incident provided a rallying point for Indian nationalists. One of them, a young man called Jawaharlal Nehru, later wrote that it revealed "how brutal and immoral imperialism was."

The deed also shocked British liberal opinion: Following an inquiry, the British commander at Amritsar, General Dyer, was dismissed. But the British reaction to the slaughter at Amritsar came too late to still Indian outrage. Nationalism was no longer confined to a tiny, educated minority: It had become a mass movement. And it had acquired an extraordinary leader.

Mohandas Karamchand Gandhi, later known universally as the Mahatma, "Great Soul," was born in 1869 to a high-caste Gujarati family. From the beginning, he was a man of two worlds, the old and the new. His background was intensely traditional, but he defied orthodoxy by crossing the ocean to study law in London. In 1893, he traveled to South Africa to undertake some legal work. A week after his arrival, he was evicted from a first-class railroad coach, because of his color, by a white ticket inspector. Radicalized by this experience, Gandhi spent the next 21 years in South Africa, skillfully opposing laws that discriminated against Indians. He developed a strategy of nonviolent civil disobedience: the movement called *satyagraha,* which literally means "insistence on truth." His campaigns greatly embarrassed the South African government and attracted a good deal of world attention—including, ironically enough, the fulsome praise of the British viceroy of India.

Gandhi returned to India after the outbreak of the war, and by 1918, he was the leading personality in the Congress movement. His legal skills enabled him to talk to the British in their own terms; the simplicity of his life and his saintly eccentricity, both in the tradition of India's gurus, appealedto the masses. It was fortunate for everyone that his teachings were nonviolent.

Even so, thousands died in each of the three great campaigns he launched between the end of World War I and Independence. The first, from 1920 to 1922, attempted to include the Muslim community in what was threatening to become a largely Hindu movement. Curiously, the issue that was chosen to bring the two communities together came from Turkey, where in the aftermath of the war, the Allies were threatening to eliminate the sultan. As the embodiment of the ancient Islamic caliphate, he was a figure of great spiritual importance to Muslims. Thus the 1920 campaign combined *swaraj* agitation with procaliphate protest. It showed how effective his techniques of civil disobedience could be in making India ungovernable.

Nevertheless, it misfired badly. In the end, the caliphate was abolished—not by the Allies but by the Turks themselves, as a symbol of reactionary tyranny. And far from promoting intercommunal harmony, the campaign only roused religious passions to an extent that led to serious intercommunal violence. Gandhi was horrified by the bloodshed and called off the protest, which was easier said than done.

The British jailed him in 1922 on a charge of sedition, releasing him two years later. For a time, he devoted himself to less obviously anti-British activities: a campaign against the low status of Hindu Untouchables—his lifelong passion—and a great effort at rural regeneration, based on handcrafts.

Gandhi's next civil disobedience campaign was in 1930. It took the form of a 250-mile trek to the coast to gather a handful of sea salt, in defiance of a government monopoly of the commodity. After flouting the law himself, Gandhi urged Indians everywhere to help themselves to natural salt. The aim of the judicious lawbreaking was to compel the British into a mass-arrest policy that would first embarrass and then paralyze the Delhi government.

It was highly effective. The outcome was a series of talks that led to the 1935 Government of India Act, which created a federal constitution with full provincial autonomy, and a complex system of British-Indian power sharing at the center. The Act, though, was less a negotiated deal than a unilateral British concession; it left Congress unsatisfied, deeply suspicious and barely willing to participate in the elections that followed in 1936 and 1937.

Congress, in fact, had come to think of itself not as an independence movement but as a government-in-waiting, whose only problem was the obdurate refusal of the British to pack up and go. As a result, it made the fateful mistake of underestimating the forces of Muslim separatism.

The Muslims too had found a leader: Muhammad Ali Jinnah, like Gandhi a Bombay lawyer by profession. Jinnah had resolved to transform the chronic Muslim fear of Hindu domination into a well-organized campaign for a sepa-

3

In September of 1947, six weeks after the British departure from India, a train packed with refugees leaves Delhi bound for the new Muslim state of Pakistan. More than seven million Muslims fled to Pakistan after Partition; 40 million remained in India.

rate Muslim state—Pakistan—after the inevitable end of British rule. His prospects of success looked slim, since the idea appalled the British. The Congress party refused to take it seriously. Indeed, it might never have come to pass had the steady devolution of British power continued as most parties foresaw. In September 1939, however, war broke out in Europe.

At once, the viceroy declared war on Germany on India's behalf. Outraged at the lack of consultation, the Congress politicians who had formed provincial ministries after 1937 resigned *en masse*. Jinnah was overjoyed: He declared "a day of deliverance and thanksgiving" and used the constitutional vacuum to forward the cause of separatism.

In 1942, after Japan's entry into the war had brought India into the front line, the British offered India the prospect of postwar self-government, and declared that provinces might, if they chose, contract out of the federation—a concession to the Muslim League that Congress found intolerable. Besides, the war situation was critical: As Gandhi put it, what use was "a post-dated check on a crashing bank"? And even if Britain did not lose the war, there was always the chance that it could be induced to concede all Congress' demands. Congress rejected the offer, and with it the last chance of Hindu-Muslim reconciliation.

The rejection was backed up by Gandhi's last campaign. Its slogan was "Quit India!" and it was, in his words, "open rebellion." As for the Japanese, then massing on India's frontier, the Mahatma was sanguine. "The presence of the British in India is an invitation to Japan to invade India," he declared in his own newspaper. "Their withdrawal removes the bait."

Gandhi's theory was never put to the test. The British reacted vigorously to the campaign, imprisoning not only him but the entire Congress leadership and many thousands of the rank and file. Hundreds died in the ensuing riots, but "Quit India" was a failure. The British did not go, and until 1945, most of Congress languished impotently in jail while the Muslim League grew from strength to uncompromising strength.

Nonpolitical India got on with the war. Without conscription, the Indian Army grew fourteenfold, to more than two million troops—many led by Indian officers—and fought in most theaters. After the initial British defeats in Asia, a predominantly Indian force stopped the Japanese offensive in the jungles of Assam. Side by side, Indian and British troops retook Burma.

Meanwhile, Subhash Chandra Bose, a leading Indian politician and president of Congress from 1938 to 1939, became the focus of Indian opposition to Britain. Escaping house arrest in 1941, he traveled to Germany to a warm welcome by Hitler. He broadcast from there to his countrymen, urging them to revolt against the British. Later on, he formed the 60,000-strong Indian National Army from troops captured by the Japanese. This Japanese-backed force was really a propaganda weapon: In combat with the regular Indian Army, it simply melted away. It was a warning to the British, however, that they could no longer count on the reliability of the armed men who upheld their rule.

But by 1945, there was no question of British rule continuing—the principle of independence had been conceded in 1942, and there was no going back. The problem was not whether to grant independence, but how.

For the gap between the Muslim and Hindu communities had become a chasm. Although the viceroy was able to form, for a time, a joint Congress-League "government," it was less a working coalition than a platform for irreconcilable differences. Far worse, the tensions between leaders were paralleled on the streets of Indian cities by the most murderous outbreaks of intercommunal violence so far. The killing gradually spread from the cities to rural areas. By the end of 1946, law and order—for long the proudest boast of the British raj—were disappearing fast, and the subcontinent was perilously close to anarchy. True to his principles of nonviolence, Gandhi toured affected areas at great personal risk and used his authority to calm enraged mobs.

In February 1947, the British government, hoping that a definite deadline would pressure the rival leaders into agreement, declared June 1948 as their departure date. To implement their decision, they sent a new viceroy: Lord Louis Mountbatten, who was not only a successful wartime commander but a member of the British royal family. At his own request, Mountbatten was given full plenipotentiary powers, and almost at once, he proceeded to use them. Partition, he recognized, was now inevitable. By May 1947, with no foreseeable end to the bloodshed, even Congress agreed. In June of 1947, Mountbatten went further. The British would leave, he announced, not in 1948 but in six weeks' time. Any longer, he reasoned, would only give extremists more time to organize.

Mountbatten may well have been right. The immediate result, however, was that the last days of the British raj were a frenzied scramble, in which boundaries were determined and the

assets of the old government of India, from its army to its gold reserves, were hurriedly divided between two new and antagonistic nations.

In Punjab and in Bengal, where Hindu and Muslim populations were hopelessly intermingled across the new frontiers, the refugee problem was immense. By the million, Muslims and Hindus uprooted themselves and fled from each other in terror. Many did not escape. Estimates of the death toll ranged from 200,000 to two million: The vagueness of the figures gives a chilling picture of the convulsions that marked the birth of India and Pakistan.

Amid scenes of unbridled joy, the formal transfer took place in Delhi on August 15, 1947. The departing British exchanged effusive compliments with the incoming Indian provisional government, led by Nehru, who had told a French journalist in 1946: "When the British go, there will be no more communal trouble in India."

Unfortunately, there was a great deal of trouble still to come. The Indian princes had been warned that, with the end of British rule, they would have to accede to either India or Pakistan; most had done so. However, the Nizam of Hyderabad and the Maharaja of Kashmir, rulers of the two largest princely states, were reluctant to surrender their independence. A Pakistani invasion of Kashmir led to the Maharaja's belated accession to India, the arrival of Indian troops and the first Indo-Pakistani war—a major cause of the intense rivalry that would attend future relations between the two states. In the tradition of the British raj, Nehru organized a rapid "police action," which brought Hyderabad into the Indian fold.

In Delhi itself, in the months after Independence, a new wave of communal violence threatened to destroy the city: Only the desperate efforts of Gandhi, now in his 78th year, brought the situation under control. He began a fast, which he refused to break until the leaders of the city's rival communities had agreed to work together for peace. It was the last, and one of the greatest, of the services the Mahatma performed for the ideals to which he had devoted his life. In January 1948, enraged by Gandhi's attempts to defend Delhi's beleaguered Muslims, a Hindu fanatic emptied a revolver into his frail body. All over the subcontinent, Indians mourned the beloved leader who had led them to freedom. □

An Indian Railways inspector is trundled past the Taj Mahal as he checks the track for the world's fifth-largest rail network. Some inspectors' carts are gas powered, but many rely on human muscle: The men push the vehicle up inclines, then jump aboard and ride with it on the downhill stretches.

CONFIDENT STEPS OF A NEW NATION

He comes from his fields on the baking northern plain, hitching up his dhoti as he trudges the dusty road. He emerges from the scented, lush plantations of the south. He walks from the rice paddies and the forests and the ocean coasts. He draws his warm cloak around him as he marches down the mountain passes of the Himalayas. He squeezes into an overloaded bus or clambers onto an oxcart. He becomes the third passenger on a bicycle. From field and factory, humble hut or grand bungalow, he is on his way to vote at one of the 450,000 polling stations across the land. With his wife, his sons, his daughters, he is taking part in an election in the largest of the democracies. He is not only a participant in a great drama and spectacle; he is also part of a national reaffirmation of faith in a compelling hope and dream.

Indians take their politics seriously. Election campaigns are vigorous. Most politicians get close to the people in a grueling round of rallies and whistle-stop meetings. They make speeches under shady trees, or in a stadium or park, listen to local grievances, then head for the next place—where their advance men have drummed up a crowd. More than 380 million people are eligible to vote. Ballot papers are prepared in 15 different languages, and for those unable to read, each party has an easily recognized symbol.

Considering the complexities, rivalries and diversity of Indian society, with its tangled politics and numerous languages, its paradoxes and sheer scale, an Indian election is one of the wonders of the world. Many newly independent countries proclaim an allegiance to the democratic ideal but fail to sustain it. In India the ideal—even if imperfectly realized—endures.

On August 14, 1947, shortly before the midnight hour of India's Independence, Jawaharlal Nehru, one of modern India's master builders and its first prime minister, voiced his emotions and touched those of India's citizens with a historic promise.

He spoke in Delhi, the capital city built on an ancient crossroads of the northern plains. "Long years ago," he said, "we made a tryst with destiny, and now the time comes when we shall redeem our pledge, not wholly or in full measure, but very substantially. At the stroke of the midnight hour, while the world sleeps, India will awake to life and freedom. . . . A moment comes, which comes but rarely in history, when we step out from the old to the new, when an age ends, and when the soul of a nation, long suppressed, finds utterance. . . . We have to build the noble mansion of free India where all her children may dwell."

Nehru knew as he spoke that the road ahead would be hard. His country was vast and poor, economically stagnant, vulnerable to drought and famine, torn by communal tensions. Most of the land was still run on feudal lines.

4

Prime Minister Jawaharlal Nehru and his daughter, Indira Gandhi, confer during a meeting of the Congress party in 1962. After his death, Mrs. Gandhi compared their styles: "My father was a statesman, I am a political woman. My father was a saint. I am not."

Political, economic and social problems were immense. The British had ruled India largely to suit their own economic interests. Native industries had been developed only patchily, and factories were mostly devoted to cotton and jute processing. Although two thirds of the population worked on the land, India did not produce enough food to feed itself. Not much had been done for the education and health of the people. The majority of children did not attend school, and only about 15 percent of the population could read or write. There was a high incidence of diseases such as smallpox, malaria and cholera.

On the positive side, though, India had tremendous reserves of raw materials and plentiful human resources. It inherited a useful railroad network, a well-run legal system, and a disciplined and competent body of civil servants imbued with ideals of public service. Apart from a great famine in Bengal in 1943, the country had not been ravaged during World War II.

Through all the years of the Independence struggle, Gandhi and other leaders had argued against clearing the decks by violent revolution and proposed instead a policy based on selflessness and cooperative progress. At Independence, they embraced democracy as a way of managing India's heterogeneous society and strengthening the ideal of national unity. The British parliamentary system was admired—and eventually imitated. In the Indian Parliament today the lower house, the Lok Sabha, has seats upholstered in Westminster green, as in the House of Commons in London. The seats of the upper house, the Rajya Sabha, are as red as those in the House of Lords.

On January 26, 1950, India changed its status from a dominion in the British Commonwealth to a full-fledged republic, although it remained a member of the Commonwealth. The 1950 Constitution is still in force. It made India a union of states with a strong federal center to prevent fragmentation. Each state has an elected legislature headed by a chief minister. The Parliament in Delhi has a directly elected lower house and an upper house mostly elected by the state legislatures.

The states and central government divide up legislation. States enact their own laws on education, public health and local taxes, while the center deals with defense and foreign policy. In a number of other areas, such as economic and social planning and trade-union law, the center and the states share power; but the center generally has the last word.

India has a large number of political parties. Coalescing around a leader with a strong personality, they come into being at a bewildering pace and splinter apart equally rapidly. Many of the parties in both the central and the state parliaments have a regional basis: They may represent language groups or alliances of certain castes.

All of India's parties are small in comparison with the dominant political machine, the Congress party, which before 1947 was the focus of the independence movement. The party has held on to power for all but three of the post-Independence years; to make any headway against it, its smaller opponents must unite in a coalition. Congress also dominates many of the state parliaments. Its preeminence derives partly from its long history and its role in securing independence, partly from the strong organization it has built up in every state and partly from its succession of charismatic leaders—Nehru the visionary nation-builder, his daughter Indira Gandhi and his grandson Rajiv Gandhi.

India was fortunate to have Nehru as leader during its first years of independence. He had his dream, and he communicated it. As he said, "It is not enough for us merely to produce the material goods of the world. We do want high standards of living, but not at the cost of man's creative spirit, his creative energy."

A natural institution-builder, Nehru loved Parliament. He took it seriously, nurtured it and made it a part of India's decision-making machinery. An enthusiastic debater, he set an example as a parliamentarian.

Nehru was born in 1889; his father, Motilal Nehru, was a wealthy and brilliant lawyer. Jawaharlal was educated in the manner of a young English gentleman, at Harrow, one of Britain's leading private schools, and then at Cambridge University. Although he emerged with a distinctly Western outlook and taste, his experiences did not erode his strong Indian core, nor his pride in his country.

He was of the highest caste grouping, a Brahmin. He followed no religion and professed a dislike for the title of Pandit—a Hindu honorific meaning "learned one"—which the people bestowed on him. Intellectually gifted and energetic, he had a charm and eloquence that captivated people, from the highest to the humblest. By the time independence was granted, he was a seasoned politician, having been the Mahatma's right-hand man and four times president of Congress.

The new India that Nehru led called itself a democratic socialist secular republic. As it turned out, the Congress

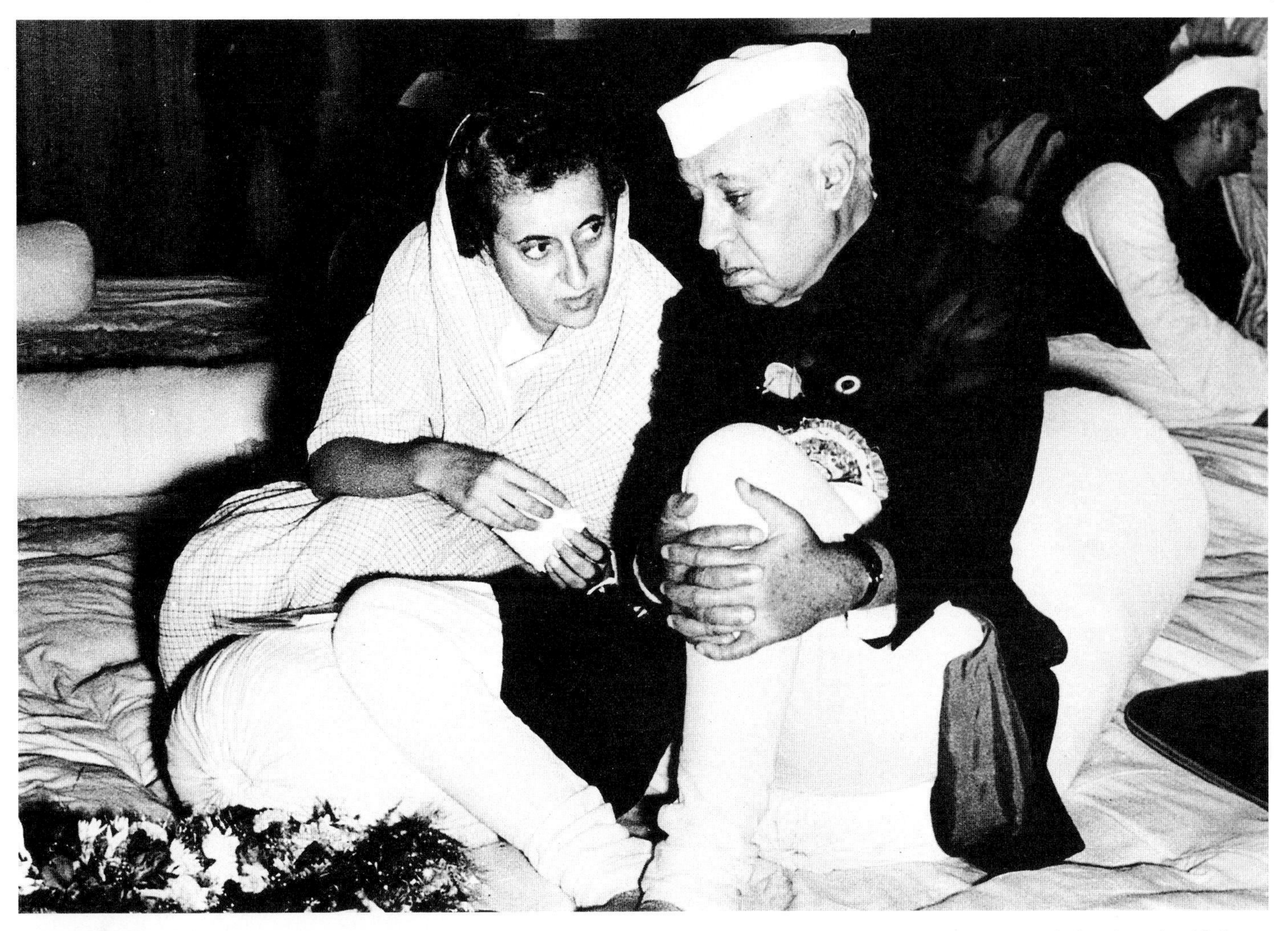

party did not adopt an unqualified socialist policy. Even in the 1950s, its most left-wing period, it included a strong conservative element. Nehru himself was a Fabian, an intellectual democratic socialist, who had beliefs that were rooted in the fashionable ideas of the 1920s and 1930s. In his sort of socialism, capital was to be controlled in the national interest. Economic development was to be planned and coordinated from the center so that all would benefit. But he was antiauthoritarian and had rejected Marxism after having seen it in action in the Soviet Union. Nehru had also rejected Gandhi's concept of a nonindustrial society rooted in rural democracies, because he thought that such a system would do nothing to raise people from their poverty.

Nehru believed in a strong public sector, with state-owned steel, power, manufacturing, mining and transportation occupying the commanding heights of the economy. He envisioned mighty industrial plants as the temples of modern India. He made economic self-reliance a national cause. In 1951, the first in a series of five-year plans was launched. Nehru was to preside over three of them. The outcome was a mixture of success and disappointment, with some conspicuous failures.

Under the first five-year plan, India took steps toward freeing itself from the burden of having to import food. Irrigation systems and fertilizer plants were started. Some of Nehru's temples of industry came into being. Three large steel plants were built, and power projects were put into motion. Nehru was like a master of ceremonies, traveling the country to open dams and factories. Optimism was in the air, and Indians had a strong sense of moving forward. The annual growth rate averaged more than 4 percent between the start of the 1950s and 1964.

The emphasis was on the public sector, but parts of the private sector also did well, notably the businesses of the

Tata and Birla families. The Tatas had started out in the 19th century in cotton and silk, the Birlas in the early years of this century in cotton and jute. By Independence, both families were running huge conglomerates with a vast range of interests, which expanded still further in the decades that followed.

The second plan emphasized heavy industry, and the third promoted agriculture. Neither was matched by reality; the targets of the third plan in particular had to be sharply trimmed. The disarray was so bad that the fourth plan, due to start in 1966, was postponed. Between 1964 and 1971, the annual growth rate was down to an average of 3 percent.

A major problem was the lack of capital. The government had to tax and borrow to raise the money for investment. But although tax rates were high, tax revenues were limited because most Indians were poor and were able to save little, if anything.

The weather also had a good deal to do with the poor results. In the early postwar decades, before extensive irrigation systems had been completed, India was far more dependent on the annual rains than it is today. During the period of the first five-year plan there were three good harvests; but poor monsoons, leading to regional famine and rationing, blighted both the second and third plans. With hindsight it can be seen that, even granted more capital and better weather, the plans were too ambitious. High hopes had become high targets. Nehru's commitment was total, but his ideas were too general and he did not pay enough attention to making things work.

His insistence on a large public sector sowed many seeds of trouble. There were compelling arguments for strong state involvement in industry in its early days: the state could ensure that the basic infrastructure was laid in place, whereas a private free-for-all might have provided consumer goods for the rich while leaving damaging gaps in the basic industries. But inefficiency and corruption spread. In India, it is not considered shameful to use one's position to help relatives and other members of one's caste by finding them jobs. Inevitably, state industries, sheltered from competitive pressures, took on more staff than they needed, as did the government departments set up to direct the economy. Bribery circumvented delays caused by excessive bureaucracy. The pay of government clerks was—and remains—very low, so temptation was great. The shortcomings of the nationalized industries resulted in a continuing drain on resources. The country's scarce capital was squandered, and the potential growth rate was not achieved.

Nehru set out not just to produce wealth, but also to improve education and health and to make the country a more equal society. His efforts in education met with mixed results; the gains were most impressive at the highest level: He established many universities and technical colleges. By the 1980s, approximately 8 percent of Indians in their early twenties were enrolled in higher education and India boasted the third-largest number of science graduates of any country. Admittedly, degrees in some Indian universities are not equivalent to those granted by Western establishments, but the best scholarship is very good indeed. The country has produced five Nobel prizewinners since Independence.

Under Nehru, primary education was made compulsory; but it has always been easy to evade the legal requirement and, today, nearly one fifth of primary-age children do not go to school. Some of those who do attend may find themselves in a brick schoolhouse, but many learn their lessons under a thatched awning, or simply sitting under a shade tree.

The battle against disease has been waged effectively. Inoculation reduced such scourges as cholera and eliminated smallpox altogether, although tuberculosis, leprosy and dysentery are still serious problems. Spraying land with DDT all but conquered malaria by the 1970s, but the disease began to return in the 1980s.

Disease control and public-health improvements contributed to a steady increase in the population. Even in 1947 India was a populous country, with land at a premium. In the 1950s, population growth was not considered a serious problem; the priority was seen as growing crops more efficiently to feed everyone. After the 1961 census had revealed the pace of growth, birth-control clinics were set up across India. They made some inroads into population growth, but progress was slow. Many rural people did not want to limit their families, and those who did often had difficulties with sophisticated contraceptive techniques or found their side effects unacceptable.

Nehru worked to erode traditions that offended his liberal and egalitarian ideas. In particular, he battled through Parliament two controversial measures that improved the position of women. These gave women equal property rights with men and the right to support payments after divorce. The vigor with which they were opposed showed the strength of traditions.

Nehru's greatest passion was foreign

POLITICAL SYMBOLS TO REACH THE ILLITERATE

A citizen of Kerala *(above)* sits beneath a hammer, sickle and star painted on a teashop wall. The emblem represents the Communist party of India — Marxist, the larger of the nation's two Communist parties. The symbols of some of the main national parties appear below.

India's medley of political parties rely as much on election symbols as on candidates or programs to establish their identities among illiterate voters. The symbol alone appears next to the candidate's name on ballots, and before a poll, campaigners popularize their emblems with handbills and posters.

The chief election commissioner invites the parties to choose neutral symbols: Some emblems, however, carry potent messages. Before 1969, the symbol of the Congress party was a pair of bullocks — India's most valued farm animals. That year, Congress split in two and the splinter parties fought bitterly over the emotive oxen. The case went to the Supreme Court, which ruled that neither group could claim the symbol. Congress' current motif, a hand, is reminiscent of the billboards of palmists; many voters probably subliminally identify it with good luck.

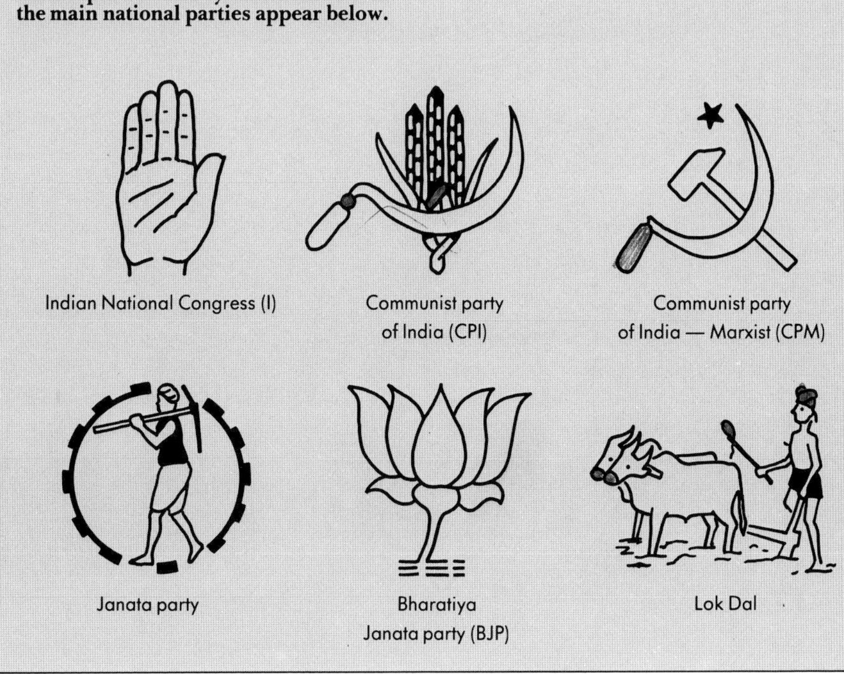

policy. He was the architect of India's foreign relations and invariably had his own way in the Cabinet. He once said: "Prime ministership is not my profession and I would have resigned but for one thing, and that is my interest in the foreign affairs portfolio." He believed India should have a full role in the world and was determined to establish its independence. Thus he was a founder in the 1950s of the nonaligned movement, along with President Tito of Yugoslavia and President Nasser of Egypt. He said he hated big-power politics and was convinced that India should remain independent of the two adversaries in the Cold War.

He saw nonalignment as the building of a third force for peace, the adoption of Gandhian ideas in foreign policy. But to Americans, Nehru seemed to be cultivating a more agreeable relationship with the Soviet Union than with the United States. The Americans were irritated by the fact that India seemed to make a habit of criticizing U.S. actions, and they were suspicious of India's socialist economic programs. They also took note of Nehru's instant condemnation of the British and French attack on Suez in 1956 and his reluctance to criticize the Soviet invasion of Hungary the same year.

The United States provided much aid to India in the form of food, and it funded loans through the World Bank. But at a time when the U.S. was not eager to provide India with industrial know-how, India turned instead to the Soviet Union, which built a steelworks and other large projects in the 1960s. The Soviets also sold India arms and aircraft. These economic links with the U.S.S.R. increased the resentment and suspicion the U.S. felt toward India, coloring the relationship between the

A giant crane heaves a girder into the air while laborers on the riverbank carry baskets of crushed stone for concrete to complete a bridge spanning the

Ganges at Patna. The 3.4-mile-long structure — Indian in design and construction — is Asia's longest river bridge; the first two lanes were opened in 1982.

4

world's two largest democracies.

But this friction was relatively minor in comparison with the calamitous crisis that finally exploded with China, India's larger and more populous neighbor to the north and east. In the late 1950s, India and China quarreled over their vague and disputed common border in the remote Aksai Chin plateau, where China and Kashmir meet. Subsequently the disagreement spread, and China contested the border in the mountainous northeast of India. The dispute was kept from the Indian people for three years, so its disclosure came as a shock. In 1962, war broke out. Chinese troops poured over India's northeastern frontier, and Indian forces fared badly in the difficult conditions. They were not properly equipped for the task: Basic necessities such as boots and blankets were in short supply. Nehru asked for, and received, defense equipment from both the Americans and the Soviets.

The Chinese eventually withdrew. They got what they wanted in Aksai Chin and left unresolved the question of frontier demarcation in the northeast. In humiliated India, there were recriminations and evidence of incompetence among the generals. The war was Nehru's greatest foreign policy failure, and he never recovered from it.

Meanwhile, the third five-year plan was not being fulfilled. The war with China diverted resources, and for two consecutive years there were bad harvests. Industrial growth had slowed, and planners became acutely aware that the rapid increase in population was eroding what gain remained.

Nehru died in Delhi on May 27, 1964, aged 74. He had been prime minister for 17 years without a break. He had seen to it that the democratic ideal was well-planted and nourished. He had created wealth in India, though not enough. His efforts to distribute the wealth more fairly, in accordance with his socialist principles, had met with little success—partly because few other politicians shared his idealism. Despite his disappointments, his achievements

were remarkable; many of them were indelible. The country mourned a giant. Close to the banks of the Jumna river in Delhi, his body was placed upon a pyre and his grandson, Sanjay Gandhi, applied the flame.

The succession was smooth. The Congress party remained in power and Lal Bahadur Shastri, a diminutive man with a flair for conciliation in the Gandhian tradition, became prime minister. The key event of his premiership was a war with Pakistan over the disputed Kashmir border, which raged in Kashmir and Punjab in August and September of 1965. Each nation took land from the other. But at the end of September, when a United Nations cease-fire was agreed on, the strategic victory was India's; Shastri's firmness had made him a national hero. He died in January of 1966, at the conclusion of the peace conference.

The Shastri period was but a short gap between the long reigns of Nehru and his daughter, Indira Gandhi. She had been information minister in the Shastri government and now emerged to contend for the leadership. Congress party bosses, known as the Syndicate, chose her because she was the consensus candidate. In private, they disparaged her as "the dumb doll," believing she would be easy to bend to their wishes. She soon showed that under her mild exterior lay a shrewd mind and a ruthless will. As Henry Kissinger wrote years later: "She has few peers in the cold-blooded calculation of the elements of power."

Indira Gandhi, born at the Nehru family home in Allahabad on November 19, 1917, was Nehru's only child. Politics and the independence struggle filled her young life. She burned a beloved toy because it was British-made and stopped wearing Western clothes. During much of her childhood, her parents and her grandfather were languishing in jail for the cause.

Indira grew up an insecure and shy girl. Her education, in India, Switzerland and Britain, was spasmodic and unsatisfactory. In London she was courted by Feroze Gandhi, a charming and handsome journalist, and they married after their return to India in 1942. It was a mixed marriage, she a Hindu, he a Parsi, and there was public criticism of it. Nehru disapproved, too. In a society of arranged marriages, this kind of love-match was unusual. It was early evidence of Indira's independent-mindedness. She gained one of the magic surnames of India (although Feroze was not related to Mahatma) and had two sons, Rajiv and Sanjay. Feroze died in 1960.

Meanwhile, in the 1950s, Indira had become an apprentice to power. Her long-widowed father asked her to be his hostess; she traveled widely with him, attended talks with national and world leaders, and had a unique opportunity to watch and learn the business of government and politics. She became Congress president in 1959.

Thus she was no novice when she took power. And she was a wily political infighter. She outmaneuvered her opponents in Congress, undermined the pompous Syndicate and obliged her supporters to break away from the rest of the Congress party, which became an impotent minority. She won a resounding victory in the 1971 general election. India acclaimed Nehru's daughter. She made herself popular, traveling extensively, being seen constantly in the villages. In the days before television had any significance, she knew the importance of her physical presence. Whenever a flood or other disaster struck, she appeared on the scene to comfort and calm the survivors. But she had a genuine interest in the village people who worked the land and who made up the bulk of India's population. She noted with pride that people called her Mother.

Her popularity reached a peak in her election year of 1971 through her handling of the war of independence in which the Bengalis of East Pakistan broke away and established Bangladesh. The inevitability of the split between Pakistan's east and west wings had been built in at Partition. The two parts were separated by distance, language and culture. All they had in common was Islam. But this cement was not strong enough to bind them.

An autonomy movement grew in the east, and in March of 1971, the Pakistan government and armed forces stamped on it with great brutality. There was a wave of killing. About nine million people, an eighth of East Pakistan's population, fled to India. Somehow India coped with the burden of feeding and sheltering the refugees. For months, Indira Gandhi resisted internal pressure to intervene militarily, although India succored Bengali insurgents, the Mukti Bahini, fighting inside East Pakistan. As tension rose, Gandhi insisted that Pakistani forces leave the east. At last the dam broke, and in December 1971, Pakistan and India found themselves at war.

The fighting lasted 12 days. The well-prepared and masterfully managed Indian forces overran East Pakistan, taking Dhaka, the capital, and making prisoners of 93,000 men of the Pakistani army. Early in 1972, the new state of Bangladesh was born out of the

Traders perched in curbside stalls outside the Calcutta Stock Exchange gather information about transactions to relay to office-bound brokers by telephone. The number of stockholders in India is growing fast: It tripled between 1980 and 1985.

4

bloody struggle. Its 80 million people were soon to endure tumult, coups and assassinations as its leaders fought out their bitter power struggles against a background of poverty, natural disasters and runaway population growth. The early democratic ideal was soon to be submerged under the rule of soldiers. But in the heady early months of 1972 there was euphoria.

For the prime minister, the episode was a vindication of her earlier restraint and subsequent confident action. Thanks to India's successful move, Pakistan was broken, split into two. But India made no territorial claims and withdrew its troops after three months. During the course of the war, India received Soviet support. The U.S. had backed Pakistan, hoping to save it from disintegration. With the war over, India and Indira Gandhi had gained in stature, U.S. policy in the area had collapsed, the Soviets were friendly and the Chinese noncommittal. Bangladesh joined the Commonwealth. Pakistan, piqued, withdrew.

Gandhi's period of power saw a great internal triumph as significant in its way as her success on the battlefield—a sharp increase in wheat and rice production. This Green Revolution of the late 1960s came about through the use of new high-yield wheat and rice strains, increased use of fertilizer and better irrigation. Initially the improvements were seen almost exclusively in the wheat-growing Punjab, but gradually they spread to other states. By the early 1970s, India was self-sufficient in grain, and by the mid-1980s it was actually exporting a small quantity of wheat. With adequate buffer stocks, the country can now face drought years without resorting to the wheat imports necessary in earlier decades.

Indira Gandhi's achievements with the rest of the Indian economy were mixed. Unlike her father, she was not committed to socialism, although she spoke of India as a socialist country. She approved in principle of entrepreneurship, but she remained suspicious of the businessmen who supported her, and for a long time she did very little to free the economy from government red tape. Quotas place limits on production; any new venture required a license. Bribery and "fixed" permits were embedded in the way of life. Industries in trouble were bailed out regardless of their potential.

The state-owned concerns, making everything from bread to shoes and ships, continued to do badly. State industries made up three quarters of India's industrial assets, yet by 1980 they were providing only one third of industrial output. Their poor performance jeopardized other concerns. The state-owned power company, for example, failed to keep up with India's

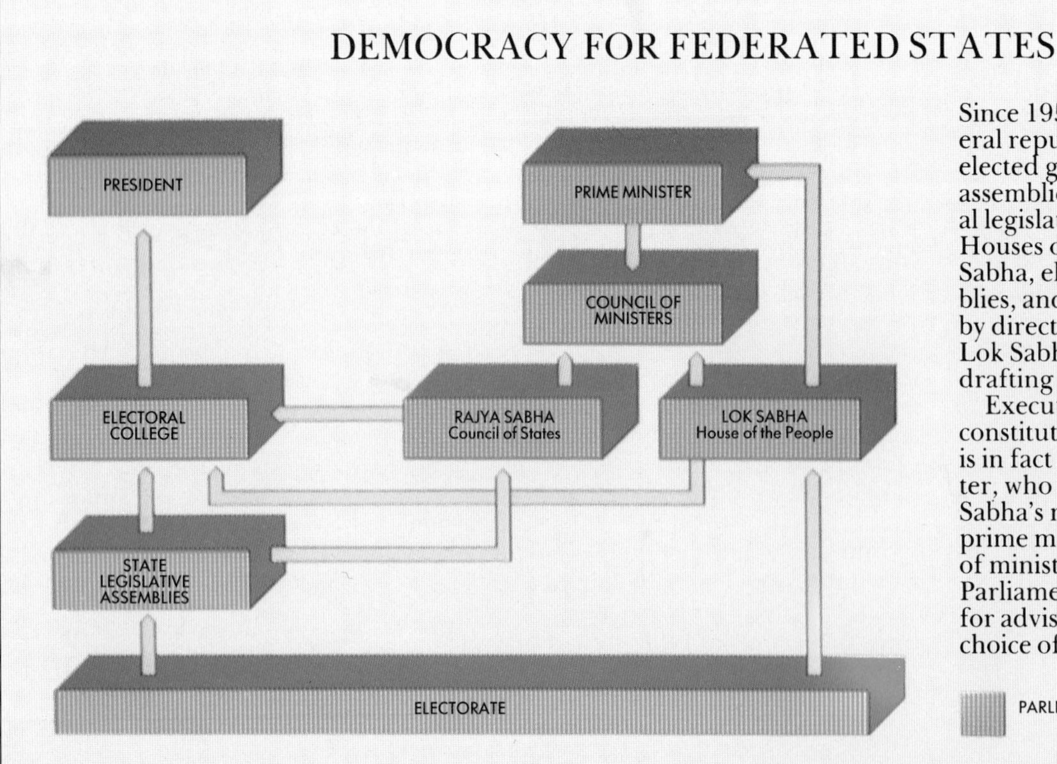

DEMOCRACY FOR FEDERATED STATES

Since 1950, India has been a federal republic with a democratically elected government and elected assemblies for its 23 states. National legislation passes through two Houses of Parliament: the Rajya Sabha, elected by the state assemblies, and the Lok Sabha, elected by direct, universal suffrage. The Lok Sabha is solely responsible for drafting all fiscal legislation.

Executive power, though vested constitutionally in the president, is in fact held by the prime minister, who is traditionally the Lok Sabha's majority leader. The prime minister chooses a council of ministers from the ranks of Parliament. He is also responsible for advising the president on the choice of state governors.

On Republic Day — January 26 — troops parade down the Rajpath, the broad avenue leading from the presidential residence to the All-India War Memorial in New Delhi. Each year, celebrations throughout the country commemorate the day in 1950 when India adopted its Constitution.

rapidly growing need for electricity. Even in the mid-1980s, most towns and cities were without power for several hours a day. Many firms bribed officials in the power company to provide an uninterrupted supply.

However, the bureaucracy could not altogether smother Indians' commercial instincts. Under Indira Gandhi, tiny businesses were multiplying and flourishing. The larger, more traditional industries—textiles, jute and tea—continued to make a substantial contribution to the economy. The construction industry prospered with the rapid growth of the cities. Large quantities of oil—though not large enough to meet the country's requirements—were extracted in Assam and off the shores of Gujarat. Chemical and engineering plants grew.

Gandhi, like her father, was committed to industrial and technical self-sufficiency. Protectionism sheltered native industries and contributed greatly to such Indian success stories as the growth of the Tata and Birla empires. A majority share of companies operating in India had to be Indian-owned—a regulation that in 1978 led the giant computer company IBM to pull out of India. Coca-Cola left India in 1977 rather than give in to government demands that it reveal its secret formula to indigenous soft-drink manufacturers; Indians took to drinking locally brewed products with such names as Thums-Up and Campa Cola.

In 1974, India detonated an atomic bomb; it had initiated a space program in 1962, and it actually launched its first satellite in 1975.

Self-sufficiency was a valuable goal in India's early years. Without protectionism the cotton industry, for example, would have been wiped out. But the

4

lack of outside competition lulled India's monopolies into lazy habits and deprived consumers of choice.

Both the good and the bad sides of self-sufficiency are illustrated by the automobile industry. For a generation, the car most readily available in India was a locally made version of the 1954 British Morris Oxford. Indians derived self-esteem from their ability to produce their own vehicles. The cars were suitable for local conditions—strong enough to withstand the rough roads and encounters with oxcarts. Also, their engines were simple—to the point that throughout India, villagers and town dwellers alike became expert at improvising auto repairs. The disadvantages were that the cars were in short supply, very expensive and not fuel-efficient. Moreover, they were made from the original dies for more than 20 years. As the dies grew progressively less exact, important parts, such as doors, no longer fit properly.

The goal of self-sufficiency saddled other industries with outdated technology. India's telephone system, for example, used equipment that had been designed in the 1940s, and the resulting difficulties in communication held back many enterprises.

In the early 1970s, long-running economic problems were exacerbated by bad monsoons and the cost of sheltering the Bangladesh refugees. To darken India's sky further, there came the oil crisis of 1973, set off when the oil-exporting countries increased prices fourfold. With the population growing by 12 million a year, India was like someone trying to swim wearing a lead belt. The stagnating economy contributed to a political crisis.

The prime minister had campaigned in the 1971 election under the slogan Abolish Poverty, but she had raised expectations without having the ability to satisfy them. The press grew more critical of her rule and so, naturally, did her political opponents—particularly Morarji Desai and Jayaprakash Narayan, both elderly and austere men of the Gandhian school. She felt increas-

In an electronics factory in New Delhi, a worker inspects the circuit board of a small computer. Although India's computer manufacturers still rely on foreign suppliers for high-technology microchips, the nation's program designers export software to the West.

ingly threatened by the protest movement, covering the political spectrum, that coalesced under Narayan.

In 1975, the public mood grew angry and brittle. Events came to a head in June with a court ruling in Allahabad, home of the Nehrus. The high court there annulled Gandhi's election to Parliament, ruling her guilty of malpractice in the 1971 campaign: She had used staff on the government's payroll to help in the election. The opposition demanded her resignation and called for a national civil-disobedience campaign for June 29. With the support of her younger son, Sanjay, she resolved to fight. On the night of June 25 she struck, ordering that her opponents and critics be imprisoned or placed under house arrest; the next day, she declared a state of emergency. Even the Cabinet did not know what had happened. The emergency, suspending basic rights and freedoms, was validated by Parliament, where the Congress party had a two-thirds majority. Indira Gandhi began to rule by decree. The swiftness and the completeness of the coup were stunning.

Gandhi felt she was the only one equipped to deal with India's crisis, and she acted ruthlessly on this conviction. The disturbances before the emergency were not so serious as to jeopardize India's long-term stability. But they could have led to her overthrow, and this she was not prepared to tolerate.

Many Indians welcomed the emergency. They accepted the prime minister's assertion that it was necessary for the salvation of democracy, public order and security. They felt that liberty had been abused in the preceding years. They were in the mood for self-chastisement and were pleased with the smack of firm government. Civil servants seemed to be working harder. The end of agitation in the factories was helpful to business. A crackdown on black-marketeers, hoarders and smugglers was widely applauded by honest citizens. And as luck and the monsoon would have it, there were two good harvests in succession, so food prices stabilized. India appeared to be on a more even keel.

But there was a darker side as well. People were detained without trial. The police, tough and frequently brutal, were more high-handed than ever. Many people felt that they were being spied on and were afraid to speak freely. The press was muzzled. Strikes were banned. And, meanwhile, growing ever more arrogant, were Sanjay Gandhi and his circle of activists.

Sanjay was leader of the Congress youth wing, but otherwise he had no formal office. It did not matter. He was his mother's only trusted confidant, and he acted as her manager and fixer. Ruthless and manipulative, he despised routine politics and politicians. His speeches had populist appeal. To many who watched his astonishing rise, he seemed to pose a greater threat to India than the emergency itself.

He had no political ideology. He was committed instead to modernizing India in a hurry, and supporters hailed him as "India's man of tomorrow," the man who would get things done. He urged people to plant trees, to clear the slums, to end the tradition of brides bringing a dowry to their new husbands. And he waded enthusiastically into a new campaign to reduce the population by sterilization. Previously, men had been encouraged to volunteer for a vasectomy by the promise of a gift such as a transistor radio. Now there was a determined sterilization drive, and its harshness spread terror. In certain instances, vasectomies were carried out forcibly. There are no reliable estimates of the number of forced vasectomies, but stories of ill-treatment and coercion spread rapidly across northern India, causing fear and resentment. Men fled at the sound of a jeep, for jeeps are official vehicles. Sanjay's slum-clearance campaign was also badly handled. Bulldozers roared into the old quarter of Delhi without any consideration for residents.

India's new regime was much criticized in the West, and many Indians felt humiliated. They had been intensely proud that their nation, unlike the rival Pakistan, was a democracy. Now they had lost face. But Indira Gandhi had no wish to rule as a permanent dictator. In March 1977, after 19 months of the emergency, she called a general election in the belief that she would win. She was wrong. Indians were angry about the sterilization and slum clearance, the jailings and censor-

In preparation for an exploratory flight into the upper atmosphere, technicians at the Thumba Launching Station in Kerala position a rocket for take-off. Started in 1962, India's space program is now the largest in the developing world.

In the mineral-rich state of Bihar, the chimneys of the vast Tata Iron and Steel Works spew out smoke as the morning shift arrives. India's first large-scale steel plant opened in 1907; today, there are six, of which this is the only one in the private sector.

ship. They threw her out of office. A group of opposition parties known as the Janata coalition was swept to power. The new prime minister was Morarji Desai, Gandhi's old rival, who had been detained throughout the emergency.

The amazing defeat of Indira Gandhi, and the euphoria that surrounded the return of democracy, temporarily disguised the Janata's lack of workable policies. The coalition parties had no common position apart from their dislike of the former prime minister, and no tradition of working together. Soon, irreconcilable differences between the various groups began to show up. While the Janata squandered the opportunity it had for making its government a turning point in the Indian story, Gandhi assiduously rebuilt her support. In the 1980 general election, 33 months after losing power, she and the Congress party took power again. India is Indira, Indira is India: So went the campaign slogan. It was a remarkable comeback.

But triumph was soon soured by personal tragedy. In June 1980, Sanjay Gandhi was killed, at 33, while attempting an aerobatic stunt not far from his home in Delhi. India was never to see how he would have used his position had he entrenched himself even closer to the center of power. Many were relieved. Sanjay had cast an ominous shadow. His young and ambitious followers were devastated; without him, they were nothing.

Rajiv Gandhi lighted the pyre of his younger brother. Inevitably, in the weeks and months that followed, Rajiv moved closer to his stunned mother and into the position Sanjay had occupied. Until then, Rajiv had been a pilot with Indian Airlines and had shown no interest in politics. But he recognized his mother's need for him now. Insecure despite her popularity, she had total trust only in her close family.

Determined to brook no opposition, Indira Gandhi habitually kept those of ability at a distance in her governments. Her Cabinets were notoriously weak. She gave sycophants jobs in the party machine. She did her utmost to make Congress her own instrument, undermining the party that was the essence of India's political vitality. She also resented opposition parties controlling any of the state assemblies. Wanting no regional bosses to challenge her, she managed to install puppet leaders in many regional centers.

During the early 1980s, at a time when she was riding high at home and consolidating her international image with foreign tours and her leadership of the nonaligned movement, she found herself in serious trouble with the Sikhs of Punjab. Sikhs were in the majority in that state, though just barely. The dominant group of Sikhs, the Jats, had its own political party—the Akali Dal—but it rarely won power in Punjab because the non-Jat Sikhs, like the state's Hindus, tended to vote for Congress. In 1982, the Akali Dal launched a series of anti-Congress demonstrations in Amritsar. Among the specific demands was that Chandigarh, the capital city that Punjab shared with the state of Haryana, become exclusively the capital of Punjab—but what the Akali Dal leaders really wanted was some form of permanent hegemony in Punjab.

Meanwhile, Sikh fundamentalism was growing. Ironically enough, the Congress party was partly responsible for this development, for in order to destabilize the Akali Dal, it had pushed into prominence a Sikh religious extremist named Jarnail Singh Bhindranwale. As his popularity grew, his followers began to kill Hindus. Terrorism provoked repression. Bhindranwale fled to the sanctuary of the Sikhs' holiest place, the magnificent Golden Temple in Amritsar. By 1984, he had overtaken the moderate Akali leaders as the voice of Sikh protest. Demand grew for a semiautonomous or totally separate Sikh state. Terrorism and repression escalated.

Had Gandhi acceded earlier to some of the Akali Dal's demands, a crisis might have been avoided. But she had cut herself off from good advice, and she misjudged her response to the admittedly fearsome Punjab troubles. Her usual technique of waiting, hoping that the troublemakers would tire, now proved ineffective. The presence of strongly armed Sikh extremists in the Golden Temple became an affront. The prime minister could not afford to show weakness in the face of this challenge to her authority. Although she knew the grave dangers in showing force, she sent the army, in June 1984, to crush the extremists in the Golden Temple. It was a bloody episode—and a turning point in India's history. The troops used tanks and mortars, so strong was the resistance. The fanatical Bhindranwale was among the hundreds who were killed in the bitter fighting. The assault on the temple caused a roar of outrage. Even moderate Sikhs, who detested the terrorists, were furious and hurt. The Sikh people were badly bruised, and Punjab lay sullen under martial law.

Among the extremists, there were those who vowed revenge.They would not rest until Indira Gandhi paid with her life for the assault on their holiest place. On October 31 of that year,

Ghandi was gunned down by her Sikh bodyguard as she walked from her home to her office in Delhi. Her murder provoked a terrible bout of vengeful rioting as Hindus burned Sikh homes and shops and killed more than 1,000 Sikhs. The turmoil of Punjab and the wounds of the Sikhs were to become part of Rajiv Gandhi's inheritance.

Indira Gandhi was 66 years old when she died. Her place in history remains a matter of controversy. She is blamed for weakening her party, for suspending democracy for nearly two years, for allowing corruption to thrive, for slow economic progress. Yet to lead such a huge and complex country was clearly a task that required outstanding strength. She had a remarkable relationship with the people, and this was the bedrock of her considerable popularity and long reign. Inside the nation and out of it, she was the best-known Indian. She embodied the idea of an India united and was a strong-willed figure on the world stage.

Rajiv Gandhi was sworn in as prime minister just a few hours after his mother's death. Then, in the general election at the end of 1984, he and the Congress party achieved a massive win, larger than his mother or grandfather had ever obtained. Rajiv Gandhi was uniquely placed: He was a Nehru, yet he was not stained by a career in politics, not connected with the emergency. He was unencumbered by political debts or ideology. He was fresh, decent and sincere. He had made plain his distaste for the dirtier side of politics, the maneuvering and backstabbing and corruption. At 40, he was young and modern-minded, a man who had grown up in independent India.

After Sanjay's death, Mrs. Gandhi clearly intended Rajiv to be her successor. As his mother's lieutenant during the last four years of her life, he learned at first hand how politics work. India's citizens accepted the choice partly because there was no alternative—the opposition parties were still tainted by the Janata fiasco—but even more because

4

he was the repository of all their hopes.

When the third generation of Nehrus took power, commentators began to speak of India's unofficial royal family; some thought they detected a conspiracy to undermine democracy. But the creation of a ruling dynasty was the result of a succession of accidents that nobody could have engineered. If Nehru's charisma had been weaker, if his daughter had handled the Bangladesh war less adroitly, if the Janata party had not bungled their opportunity, or if Rajiv had been tainted by the emergency, India's quasi-monarchy might well have disintegrated. However, the nature of Indian politics certainly helped Rajiv. Such a vast, disparate country needs a symbolic figure at its head; most politicians, having only a regional constituency, could offer him no serious competition. Here, Indians felt, was the one person who could bring about the changes and improvements they so earnestly desired, who could close the gap between Nehru's dreams and modern reality.

When Rajiv Gandhi became leader, two fifths of the people still lived below the official poverty line and the benefits of the Green Revolution had not yet reached everyone. Rapid population growth was a major obstacle to improving the lot of the poor: At the time of Independence the population was 350 million; Rajiv Gandhi's India had more than 730 million. In consequence of Sanjay's misdeeds during the state of emergency, birth control remained an extremely delicate issue and male sterilization had become a taboo subject in politics. By the 1980s, increasing numbers of women were accepting sterilization after they had borne two or three sons, but more than two thirds of the women in India were still not taking any contraceptive measures at all.

In the Punjab factory of Mahajan's, manufacturer of sports equipment, workers stitch up the leather hides of cricket balls. Such small-scale private industries — a growing sector of the Indian economy — account for nearly half the nation's industrial production.

Nehru's picture of India as an industrial giant, though disappointed in his own lifetime, was beginning to come true toward the end of Indira Gandhi's period of power. During her last years, the government loosened some of its controls over industry. Seeking to open India at last to foreign collaboration, it eased the self-reliance rules that kept imports out and went into partnership with a Japanese company to make small cars. It began to take a tougher line over the nationalization of troubled industries. The private sector grew and the public sector dwindled.

The industrial growth rate duly increased to more than 5 percent in the early 1980s. Earlier predictions that the Indian economy was doomed to stick forever at a "Hindu growth rate" had proved too gloomy. Most of the expansion was in consumer goods. In 1982, Indian production of bicycles was more than three times the 1965 level; production of motorcycles was 10 times the 1965 level. But bolder steps to free the economy were overdue.

Nehru's image of a free and just society had been damaged in his daughter's time. Democracy had survived; but corruption, long established in commerce and the bureaucracy, had spread into politics. The underground economy of undeclared dealings had grown enormously, and great sums of money were paid by influential individuals and corporations into the political parties, especially Congress. In some regions, the police were part of the system of bribery and oppression.

In the latter years of Mrs. Gandhi's leadership, when press censorship had been lifted, a new kind of critical and investigative journalism had grown rapidly. Through newspapers and newly launched news magazines such as *India Today* and *Sunday,* people were, for the first time, made aware of just how widespread were police brutality and corruption of various kinds.

Television, too, was helping to raise public awareness. Limited parts of the country had been receiving broadcasts since the 1960s, but in the mid-1980s there were scores of new transmitters that brought 70 percent of the country within range of broadcasts. Most television sets were in the cities, but the government had begun providing subsidized community sets in the countryside. Through Indian-produced comedies and soap operas, villagers could scrutinize the lifestyles of the more fortunate, and for the first time they could see the demeanor of their politicians.

Rajiv Gandhi made a determined effort from the first to improve public life. He replaced the most notoriously corrupt politicians with new faces. He aimed to sustain the economic growth of his mother's last years by freeing the economy from more of its shackles and by cutting income tax and the role of government in industry. He encouraged the private sector and sought the computers and computer expertise that would modernize industry. He did little, however, to directly benefit the poor, believing that the wealth created by economic growth would eventually trickle down to every level of society.

Technologically minded, like his grandfather Nehru, he began to revive the dream that India could become a leader among the world's industrial nations. This time the country was more experienced, more realistic, its expectations lower. It was exciting to feel that there was positive change. But, like their young leader, Indians knew that the task ahead was formidable. □

In Ahmadabad, a major textile center in the state of Gujarat, a woman pulls a length of dyed fabric from a bamboo drying rack. Cotton manufacture has long been India's largest industry; today, India ranks second in the world in the production of cotton cloth.

DAILY LIFE OF A CALCUTTA CLERK

Photographs by Pablo Bartholomew

Fifty-four-year-old Sukumar Chowdhary, a graduate in business, works as head clerk in the Department of the City Architect of Calcutta Corporation. Like millions of other middle-class Indians, he leads a frugal but fairly secure existence in which Western ways and traditional habits are inextricably mingled.

He lives with his wife, two grown sons, his aged mother and a maidservant in a brick house that his father built in an outlying suburb of Calcutta. With five rooms, the home is far more spacious than the accommodations that families who live closer to the center are obliged to accept. Sukumar's salary of $170 a month before taxes suffices to support his family and pay the servant, but leaves little to spare. Like many of his class in Calcutta, Sukumar is politically active and devotes his spare time to labor union activities and to the Socialist Unity Center of India, a Marxist-Leninist party to which he has belonged for 20 years. His daily routine unfailingly includes a discussion with his sons of issues raised by the morning newspaper.

In his office in central Calcutta, Sukumar studies a document at a desk piled with building applications. He works six days a week — officially from 10:30 a.m. to 5 p.m., although an inefficient public transportation system often delays his arrival until 11 a.m.

Sukumar and Bidyut stand with their sons, 22-year-old Subir and 21-year-old Sudip (wearing glasses). Both young men have high educational goals: The elder is working for a civil engineering diploma, the younger for a degree in business. They have decided not to marry until they have secure jobs.

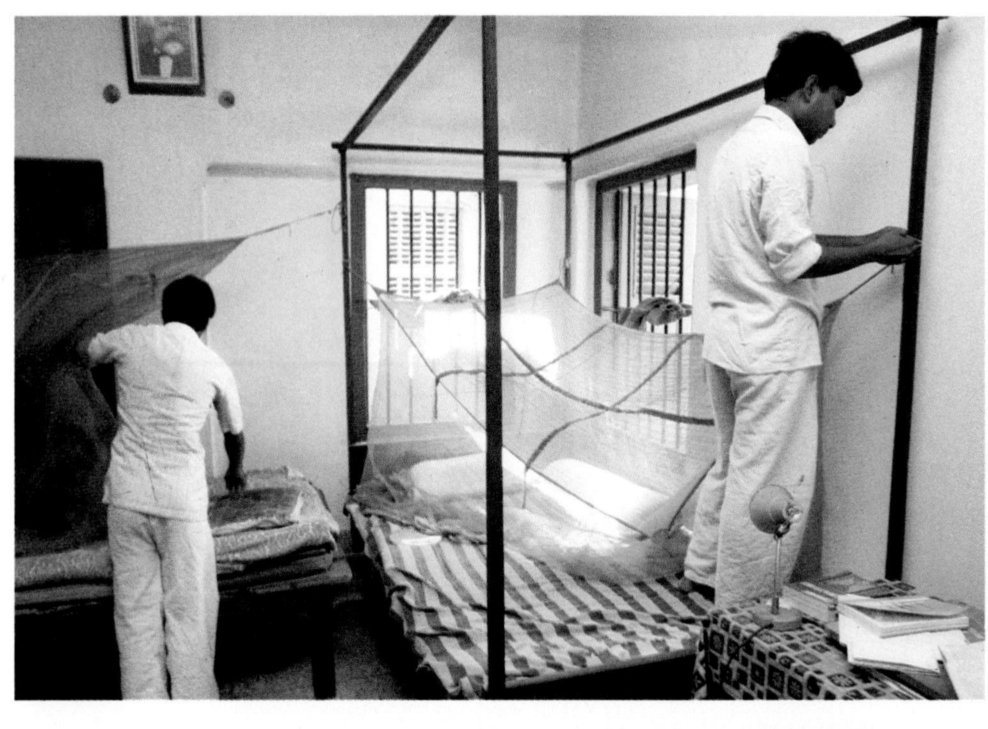

Observed from the wall by Karl Marx, Sudip and Subir dismantle the mosquito nets strung up for the night in their bedroom. When the sons marry, they will probably continue to live at home; this room will become the matrimonial quarters for one of them.

Bidyut prepares her husband's supper, crouching in the traditional manner in front of a floor-level coal burner in the spartan kitchen. The family's mainly vegetarian diet is supplemented with fish. Cooking and housework occupy much of Bidyut's day; she does not often leave the house.

Attended by their maid, the Chowdharys eat a Sunday breakfast of lightly spiced potato curry with roti, a soft bread. They sit at a table in Western fashion instead of on the floor, but following Hindu custom, they eat with the right hand. The left is used for ablutions and deemed unclean.

The Chowdharys' maidservant washes the floor of the bathroom area. The handpump beside her draws water from a well; the house is not connected to Calcutta's main water system.

On a regular shopping trip to the market before work, Sukumar buys betel leaves to make a chewy digestive called *pan*.

A bicycle-powered rickshaw, hired for a rupee or two, brings Sukumar and Subir home from market with bags of groceries. Perishables must be bought each morning, for the family does not own a refrigerator — and even if it did, Calcutta's almost daily power cuts would reduce the appliance's worth.

Dressed for work in a dhoti and loose-fitting shirt, Sukumar awaits the departure of a suburban bus from its terminus. Later, he will change to a crowded city bus that drops him off near his office. The whole commute takes approximately an hour.

In the arid northwestern state of Rajasthan, women on their way to fetch water from a communal well huddle together to protect themselves from windborne sand. Suffocating dust storms are a frequent bane in April and May, the parched months that precede the monsoon rains.

HARDSHIPS OF RURAL LIVING

As the first rays of morning sun stretch along the fields of millet and rice to light up the village of Hosahalli in the state of Karnataka, the people of each household are already moving about. While women are preparing breakfast, sweeping the house and washing pots, some of the men are walking back from the fields, where they have stayed awake all night to guard against wild pigs ruining the crops. The place is alive with noise, as people call loudly to one another, children cry, dogs bark; the clank of the blacksmith at work counterpoints the steady thud of a dozen axes splitting logs for firewood. Through the open eaves, smoke drifts upward from the cooking stoves. For breakfast, the poorest make do with a flat round of unleavened millet bread; those who can afford it also have coffee and coconut chutney.

The houses of the more than 1,000 villagers are made of roughly hewn stone and mud. Those belonging to the higher castes have tiled roofs and cement floors. Some even have stone pillars surrounding a sunken area beneath the open sky, where people wash. On the edge of the village, the mud houses of the Harijans are thatched with dried grass. Their small interiors are dark. Their owners have little or no land, and hire themselves out at a minimal daily rate to those landowners who need extra help in the fields. Each section of the village has its own well; in the middle stand the temple and the banyan tree under which the village elders have their meetings. Two small shops sell basic supplies, such as sugar, salt and tobacco. A cooperative seed store and the primary school stand at the edge of the village.

Paths radiating out from the village reach the secondary school, the distant pool for washing clothes, and the farming plots that resemble a patchwork quilt. Along the main track that leads to the neighboring village and the small town beyond, a small group of people are making their way to the market, to buy goods or to sell their produce—a handful of chilies, some green tomatoes, a basket of mangoes. An oxcart belonging to one of the wealthier farmers is loaded with melons bound for the markets of Mysore, 45 miles away. The poorest women in the village carry loads of kindling on their heads to sell to households in town: They have already walked more than five miles to the forest and back to gather and chop the firewood.

The morning sun grows stronger, burning the backs of those who work in the fields, drying the soil and ripening the crops. It is toward the end of the monsoon season—a busy time of year, for though the first rains were late, they came in sufficient abundance for the villagers to be hopeful of a reasonable harvest of rice. Those households that have small plots of lànd are striving to grow food to last them for most of the coming year. The families with plenty of land are intent on growing enough to enable them to sell a large surplus for cash: They are the ones who can afford to hire laborers from the lower castes.

All the work is done by hand. Everyone has a role dictated by age, caste and gender. The youngest children, male and female, are taking care of the sheep; older girls are helping their mothers weed the fields of millet; older boys are helping their fathers apply fertilizer. The male head of each household supervises activities; the female head of the household organizes the food supplies and doles out the right amounts to whichever of her daughters or daughters-in-law she has appointed to cook lunch that day. Those too old for heavy work in the fields are doing light jobs around the house, such as shelling beans or cleaning grit from rice. Only the children of those families where extra labor is not needed can be spared for school.

The demands of daily survival are so heavy, and the social constraints of caste and class so strong, that most households have little time or inclination to mix with others. They fear gossip, a powerful disruptive force in village life; they know how easily tensions can explode, with disputes over boundaries, grazing and water. Suspicion of other villagers and of outsiders heightens the insecurity that comes from living very close to the edge.

Hosahalli is one of India's 500,000 villages, which hold 500 million people all together—three quarters of India's population. All of them depend chiefly on agriculture or, in some cases, fishing; none have municipal administrations. Otherwise, there are no generalities that apply to all of India's villages. The fabric of rural India is like a tapestry woven with skeins of half a million shades of color: Every village is subtly

5

On a tea plantation in the state of Assam, orderly rows of workers employed by a large company move through the bushes, plucking shoots to carry back in their baskets. India is the world's largest producer of tea, and Assam grows more than half the crop.

distinguished from its neighbor and is almost totally unlike those that are set in a different climate and environment in another part of the subcontinent. In the Himalayas, the morning mist swirls around the two-story stone houses that cling to the mountainsides; in the Rajasthan desert, a mirage makes mud walls and flat roofs tremble in the heat; in Madhya Pradesh, rain water runs off thatched huts that hide in the forest; in western Tamil Nadu, avenues of tea bushes sweep down from modern bungalows on the slopes of the Nilgiri hills.

No single or multiple image can express the range of experience of village life. In a remote forest tract, a few hundred tribal people may have formed a small hamlet in a clearing and live mainly off what the forest provides. Yet on a busy highway in the northern plains, a village may grow to 10,000 people. Some villages are homogeneous, with most of the population belonging to one religion or one caste. But most villages are made up of many different religious and caste groups that, although inevitably affected by the others, keep to themselves.

Although city dwellers, whether Indian or European, often imagine Indian rural life to be frozen in time, the villages are not cut off from changes that occur elsewhere, and never have been. Since British times and even before, villages have been influenced by orders emanating from a distant administrative center: The arrival of a road or the imposition of a new rate of real estate tax may have drastic effects on a community. Neighboring villages are bound together in many different ways—through trade, through marriage, through shared services such as schools. Some villagers, at least, have always traveled away from their immediate vicinity, whether as traders, pilgrims or workers. Many peasants from Tamil Nadu migrate more than 1,000 miles to work in Delhi as domestic servants for a season or a few years.

Modernization has touched most villages, but the pace of change varies sharply. Increasingly, villagers in the outlying areas are being drawn into the towns. Some sell vegetables and firewood, some labor on building sites or roads. The more prosperous villagers go to town to buy food, such as spices or rice, and consumer goods, such as kerosene, plastic buckets and aluminum cooking pots. Yet the urban impact on a village—even one in the shadow of a town—is minimal if there is no connecting road or bus route.

Modernization means hardship for some rural people. Throughout India, artisans are losing out in the competition with inexpensive manufactured products. Weavers cannot compete with synthetic fibers and commercial prints. Papermakers, cloth printers, potters, wood carvers, basket weavers and ropemakers are all losing their livelihood. While some may depend on an uncertain export market to Western nations, many become destitute and migrate to the cities in search of work. Those who are lucky find low-paying, unskilled jobs, the men perhaps as rickshaw drivers, the women as construction workers. Having once been skilled laborers, they find their new way of life particularly hard.

Many villagers, however, have enjoyed an improvement in the quality of life, for they have been affected by a range of government programs that have reached the rural areas directly. The entire Indian countryside is divided into "development blocks" of up to 100 villages each, to which about 40 government employees are assigned. These include a dozen or more village-level workers, the last links in a chain carrying government development programs—everything from health and education to animal husbandry—to the villages.

In theory, the block officials introduce changes in consultation with the elected village assemblies called *panchayats*. These bodies, descendants of traditional councils of elders that governed village affairs, were brought into being after Independence to infuse democracy into local decision making. Few *panchayats* correspond to the democratic theory. Most are dominated by the rich landowners, and in some states, elections have not been held for years. Undermined as they so often are, the *panchayats* rarely cooperate effectively with the village-level government officials. However, the government side of the village development programs is firmly established, even if remote villages may see very little of the officials.

One of the best indicators of the programs' success is the progressive decline in infant mortality from the mid-1950s to the mid-1980s. There was only one rural health clinic for every 120 villages in the late 1980s, but immunization against common childhood diseases was gathering speed: The aim was complete coverage by the 1990s. In the early 1980s, hundreds of thousands of villages gained uncontaminated drinking water for the first time when they were provided with deep, covered wells fitted with hand pumps; by the late 1980s, fewer than 10 percent of India's villages were estimated to have an unsafe water supply.

Except in the most remote and inaccessible areas, every village had a primary school in the late 1980s. Five

times the number of secondary schools that had existed 20 years earlier were open. Two decades before, 10 percent of villages had electricity; now almost 60 percent did, bringing with it the possibility of mechanized agriculture, even if only the richer households could afford the new power source. In three decades, India had established a firm structure for improvement. The problem remaining was not so much to provide more facilities as to make them more efficient and to reach a wider range of people, particularly the poor.

Even in the areas where there seems to be least change, the elements that make up the picture are gradually altering. Oxcarts still ply the roads, but as the road surfaces improve, the large teak wheels, which are ideal for crossing uneven land, are being replaced by small wheels with rubber pneumatic tires, which are more efficient on a smooth road. Farmers still make furrows with the traditional plow pulled by two oxen, but the wooden plowshare has been replaced by one of iron. Young rural men are beginning to wear trousers instead of the traditional dhoti or lungi, and village schoolgirls nearly everywhere are now wearing machine-made skirts.

Nonetheless, village life all over India remains, as ever, attuned to the rhythm of the seasons, particularly the onset of the rains. India has two main growing seasons. Rice (the main food crop in most parts of India), corn, sorghum and millet are sown in May or June, in anticipation of the monsoon rains, and harvested in August. Wheat (the second major food crop), barley and chick-peas are sown in October or November and harvested in April. The short fallow season, September to early November, is increasingly being used for growing beans.

Traditional methods of crop production are effective in their own way. They have evolved over hundreds of years, with each generation passing on its wisdom to the next. On small plots, every inch of land is cultivated in rotation. Nothing produced is wasted: The

A row of containers await their owners' turn to draw water at a covered, hand-pumped well in a Rajasthan village. Most new bored wells are fitted with sturdy steel pumps, whose design was deliberately left unpatented to encourage the widest possible manufacture and use.

At an old-fashioned open well, a Rajasthani woman fills her water can from a bucket that she has hauled up from the well on a rope. Government workers are supposed to treat open wells with chlorine — which kills most pathogens — but in many places, treatment is haphazard.

Raised from a stone-lined waterway by a pair of yoked oxen, a bucket spills its contents down a chute and into the channels that irrigate the fields of a village in the state of Tamil Nadu.

EXPLOITING PRECIOUS SUPPLIES OF WATER

For most of India's rural population, obtaining water for irrigation and essential domestic use is a daily problem. Rivers meet some of the villagers' needs, but during the dry season, many streams dwindle to nothing. Fortunately, the water table in most parts of the country lies just beneath the surface and can be tapped by digging or boring a well.

Traditional open wells are breeding grounds for disease, but modern, machine-drilled wells are completely enclosed and the risk of contamination is reduced. Under a government project to bring clean water to every village, hundreds of thousands of such wells have been sunk since the 1970s.

pods of beans are fed to animals, and even the water in which rice has been washed is given to the oxen to provide a little nutrition.

But traditional agriculture has its drawbacks, among them the drudgery it entails. The burden is particularly heavy for women, who have the triple work load imposed by the fields, the home, and the bearing and rearing of children. Although the women guard their health, the toll shows in frequent illness and early death.

In the village of Palahalli in Karnataka, the women of one extended family work an 18-hour day, which begins at four in the morning with millet grinding—two women to a stone for more than two hours. After breakfast, the dung must be cleared and carried to the fields from the section of the house where the working cattle rest at night, safe from the possibility of theft. Then there is water to fetch and firewood to chop, the children to dress, and always a pile of clothes to wash and mend, not to mention the toil in the fields, even for those who are pregnant—planting, weeding, clearing stones, harvesting, gathering fodder and fuel. After a long day's work, there is still the rice to husk, the children to bathe, and the supper to cook and serve, before the women manage to catch a few hours of sleep, which is likely to be interrupted by children who cry or want to nurse.

The women's husbands and brothers, besides having a lighter work load, can console themselves as they labor with the reflection that the land is theirs. Pride of possession colors their attitude toward the soil. "We have great affection and trust for Mother Earth," says Bhadre Gowda, one of the men of the extended family. "When we're alive, it's she who gives us rice, gives us food. It's she who takes us in when we're dead. If we don't work the land, how will we get food?

"We worship the land. It's our life. It's beautiful. It's always beautiful. But the most beautiful is when it's green, when the crops are large and fruitful. When we cut the crops we feel empty. But then we know we'll be starting to plant again, controlling the land, making it bear fruit. And then we feel happy. We feel satisfied in working the land where we grow our life."

Bhadre Gowda and his five brothers are among the fortunate few in India's countryside who own enough land to meet their needs for food. Their father did not have any brothers, with whom he would have been obliged to share his patrimony; he inherited almost 15 acres, a large amount of land for a village farmer. Through clever timing and influence in a government office, the brothers bought other plots at a low price and practically doubled their holdings. They are now among the biggest landowners in their village, but their future is far from certain. Jealousies between the brothers threaten to divide them. They went heavily into debt to make the purchases and to develop their land: A spell of bad luck in the shape of illness or poor harvests could cost them the relative prosperity they have gained.

Less than 10 percent of the rural population are in Bhadre Gowda's position, owning enough land to be self-sufficient in food. Another 25 percent own such small plots that they must supplement their produce by working for others. Forty percent of the farming families are tenants—many of whom, again, work too little land for their requirements. The remaining 25 percent of the rural population neither own nor rent land; they eke out their living by working for others.

This very uneven distribution of land is not what had been envisaged for India at the time of Independence. Sweeping land reforms were proposed in the late 1940s and early 1950s, to abolish the landed aristocrats, or *zamindars*, many of whom were absentee landlords. The reforms were also intended to force the redistribution of land by imposing limits on the amount of land that could be held by cultivators, and to ensure security of tenure and reasonable rents for tenants.

The only part of the program to be fully implemented was the abolition, in the early 1950s, of the traditional landed aristocracy and its rights. The government bought out the *zamindars* and intended their lands to be redistributed to the small peasants. But because of loopholes in the legislation and difficulties in enforcing it, much of the newly available land went instead to those who already had plenty. Thus a new rural elite of owner-cultivators with substantial landholdings was created. They were an improvement on the past only in that they were more committed to using the land efficiently than the absentee landlords had been.

The small peasants failed to acquire much land, and tenants were never given the protection that had been proposed against eviction or extortionate rents. Each year, as the population grows and industry expands, land becomes more valuable and the small farmers grow more vulnerable. The landless laborers are even more helpless. When the reforms were proposed, it was felt unnecessary to provide them with land; their needs were to be met through various special plans for creating employment. However, these projects never materialized.

For the large numbers of the rural population who neither own nor rent enough land to sustain them, life is a constant struggle. Will there be enough paid work, not just to live but to repay the interest on debts? Will wages keep up with inflation? Will the landlord demand back his land? Their prayers are filled with requests for help, since de-

Two nurses hand out medicine from their traveling health clinic, run by a charity in Vellore, Tamil Nadu. The mobile unit regularly visits the villages within 10 miles of the medical center, and the charity trains one volunteer from each village in midwifery.

privation is a fact of everyday life. Some people become so desperate that they take on work under terms that reduce them to a state of indentured servitude, without the right to leave their employment. Although this form of exploitation has been against the law since 1976, it is estimated that in Andhra Pradesh alone there are more than 300,000 indentured laborers out of a population of 53 million. The majority are Harijans and tribal people. Many are women.

Brick kilns, stone quarries and construction sites regularly use such labor. They often send their agents on the rounds in August or September, just before the main crops are harvested, when many people in the countryside are hungry. Those who succumb, or are signed up by their families, find themselves working 12 to 14 hours a day, seven days a week, at the most grueling tasks, such as carrying loads of bricks or breaking stones. The accommodations provided for them are filthy, with no sanitation or running water. At the brickworks, the laborers often have to sleep near the blazing hot kilns even at summer's stifling peak. They have no medical facilities or assistance with child care. The wages they are promised are far from generous. Frequently, the promises are not honored and the only compensation is two meager meals a day. The workers have no redress, and if they borrow money from their employers, they are forced to stay on and work for nothing, or to put their children to work as well.

In the last three decades, the pressures bearing down on the landless have increasingly caused them to protest against the landowners, sometimes violently. The landowners have responded with more violence, and it is the poorer communities, unable to defend themselves effectively, that have suffered the most. One of the many horrifying incidents that resulted took place in Tamil Nadu in the 1960s. Farm workers seeking higher wages fought with the landowners and killed one of them. In retaliation, 300 landowners armed with guns marched on the village where the workers lived and attacked the men. Then they locked 44 villagers—mostly women and children—in a hut, doused the building with kerosene and set fire to it. Every one of the victims was burned to ashes.

While landowners all over India have been pressing their advantage, those in certain parts of the country have been using their land in new ways to create an unprecedented boom in the country's agricultural production. The boom was masterminded by the government, which was all too aware that Indian agriculture had stagnated from the early 20th century to the end of colonial rule. Part of the strategy of the newly independent nation was to grow more food. In the 1950s, output was increased mainly by expanding the areas under cultivation. In the 1960s and 1970s, a marked rise in output was achieved by increasing yields, and became part of the success story that is known as the Green Revolution. Grain production tripled between the early 1950s and the mid-1980s. And by the late 1980s, India was the fourth-largest food producer in the world.

The starting points for the Green Revolution were new dwarf wheats from Mexico and rice strains bred in Southeast Asia. Recognizing the potential of these high-yield varieties, Indian agricultural scientists introduced useful characteristics from them into Indian strains. The new Indian grains, with short stems and briefer growing seasons, yielded two to three times as much as the traditional crops. Progressive farmers quickly adopted the new technology. By the early 1980s, some 80 percent of the wheat sown and more than 50 percent of the rice sown were of the high-yield type.

The new strains were used for more than one third of India's arable land and required sophisticated techniques. Farmyard manure and compost were replaced by chemical fertilizers. By the

While women laborers bring supplies of stone rubble, men wearing rags or slippers to protect their feet from the hot tar construct a rural road. Government-funded road-building projects improve communications and create work for the rural unemployed.

Skirting a bus in the town of Jaipur, two country women head for the market to sell their produce: One bears cauliflower, the other marigolds for religious offerings. Being Hindus, they are not obliged to veil themselves in public, but country habits lead them to shroud their faces among strangers.

1980s, India was consuming more than six million tons of nitrogen- phosphate- and potassium-based fertilizers each year, and it had developed a huge fertilizer-manufacturing industry, which supplied three quarters of the demand. Pesticides also came into favor, and by the 1980s, they were protecting roughly half of the total area sown. Mechanized farming became common. From a small beginning in the 1960s, the tractor industry had increased annual production to 110,000 tractors by the mid-1980s.

The high-yield varieties are notoriously thirsty plants, and the key ingredient for the Green Revolution was irrigation. Between the 1950s and 1980s, the irrigation potential increased almost threefold, to more than 1.6 billion acres. Early efforts concentrated on storing river water in reservoirs and carrying it through the countryside in canals. But in the late 1980s, underground water, which is tapped by drilling deep wells, was as important.

Abundant underground water is to be found in Punjab, Haryana, western Uttar Pradesh, and parts of Tamil Nadu and Andhra Pradesh. This key factor, together with fertile soil, led the government to concentrate its development projects on these states, in order to achieve the fastest possible returns. The wheat-growing Punjab, Haryana and western Uttar Pradesh responded most dramatically, but the rice program, which focused on the southern states of Tamil Nadu and Andhra Pradesh, was more problematic—partly because rice requires more water than wheat, and partly because the new rice strains are prone to disease. The rice-growing poverty belt of eastern Uttar Pradesh, Bihar, Orissa, West Bengal and Assam has been untouched by the Green Revolution, despite the fact that part of this area receives so much rain that irrigation is unnecessary. Generally, the impediment to progress is that landholdings are very small, and the cash input required to transform traditional cultivation practices is too great for the farmers to risk.

In the areas blessed with underground water, the government provided easy credit for drilling tube wells—as drilled wells are known in India—so that individual farmers could get their own water supply. At the height of the Green Revolution, 20,000 new private tube wells were being sunk each year in Punjab alone. By the mid-1980s, Punjab had 600,000 tube wells, accounting for roughly half the irrigation in the state. In most of the wells, the water is pumped by electricity; some are operated by diesel engines.

An underground water supply might be expected to free farmers from dependence on monsoon rain. In fact, they still need the rain, because about 40 percent of India's electricity comes from hydroelectric power. If water behind the dams is low, there is a shortage of power to operate the well pumps. The need for electricity for irrigation is at a peak during the months of April, May and June, when it is also most in demand in the cities for refrigeration and air conditioning. The inevitable rationing means that many farmers get electricity for their wells only at night, when they cannot see to irrigate. The water from the wells is led into the fields through small channels; the farmers have to watch them closely and dam them with mud to prevent overwatering. But in the dark, the channels overflow, and the water is wasted.

Despite these difficulties, farmers who adopted the new technology have

Onions, potatoes and other winter vegetables are offered in profusion at the weekly market held in a village near Patna in Bihar. Most families grow staple grains and beans; at the local market, they supplement their needs and sell their surplus.

prospered. Newly built houses sprouting television antennas have appeared all over Punjab and Haryana. Many Indians, however, find that they are worse off as a result of the changes. The subsistence farmers and sharecroppers, who were too poor to penetrate the commercial economy, have sold out to larger landowners. Tenants have been evicted by landlords anxious to work more land and increase their profit. Many landless men have been forced to seek work in the cities or the Middle East, leaving their wives at home to hold the family together. Others have become agricultural laborers.

Even with mechanization, they find work because the high-yield varieties of grain require much attention and care. Indeed, the need for manual labor on the new varieties is such that in the sowing and harvesting seasons, thousands of migrant workers travel to Punjab from Orissa—about as far away as New York City is from Puerto Rico.

In addition to such highly visible effects on rural populations, the Green Revolution has also subtly altered the role of women in farming families. The new technology was transferred by male specialists to gatherings of village men; the women did not participate. Custom prevented them from sitting in the village meeting place with outsiders; in any case, their busy daily routine left them no time to do so. Illiteracy prevented them from reading the pamphlets that were distributed, and they lacked the freedom to travel to demonstration centers. In the past, decisions about which crops to plant, where and when to plant them, were taken by joint family councils in which the women had some say. The women still sow, weed, harvest, thresh and winnow, but as farming has become more special-

5

ized they are participating less in the crucial decisions.

The social changes engendered by the Green Revolution, whether for better or worse, have not come overnight. Tradition is a powerful force in a community as old as an Indian village, and new practices are only gradually integrated with time-hallowed customs. Akbarpur-Barota, a village in the state of Haryana with nearly 3,000 inhabitants, was introduced to the Green Revolution in the 1960s. Like most of the surrounding communities, it is an intricate mixture of old and new.

In the past, the farmers of Akbarpur-Barota grew subsistence crops of sugar cane, wheat, chick-peas, corn. Ever since electricity began transforming agriculture in the mid-1960s, they have grown the new wheat varieties almost exclusively. They sell most of the crops and buy beans and sugar in the market.

These days, diesel-operated and electric pumps are scattered all over their land. Tractors have replaced bullocks for plowing. Oxcarts have given way to trucks, bicycles, and tractors with trailers. But a number of agricultural operations are still done manually. Straw and green fodder are cut mainly on machines operated by hand. Some villagers still thresh their crops in the age-old way by hitting them against a stone. The only household activity in which labor has largely been replaced by machines is grinding: Three of the villagers own grinding machines, and they lease them to their neighbors.

Most people in the village have a lot more to eat than before. Moreover, the free primary school is well attended, unlike those in poorer communities. Many of the village boys and girls have continued their education through to middle and secondary school. Some farmers have indulged in home improvements—extending their houses, replacing a semipermanent dwelling of mud with a more permanent brick structure, or sinking private wells to lessen the women's burden.

However, few novelties have appeared inside the houses, apart from one or two gadgets, such as electric tea kettles and fans. The rich farmers spend more on hired help than before, so as to spare their women the work in the fields. Otherwise, they have invested their wealth in projects for the future—such as buying improved farm machinery or sending a son to college. The education fees are not very expensive, but the cost of maintaining a child away from home puts a severe strain on the resources of most families.

Thanks to education and the new technology, status is more and more determined by income rather than by caste. Most of the village is accounted for by five castes; some other castes, such as the barbers and potters, are represented by a few families. There are also some tribal nomadic herders and a few Muslims. The different castes live in separate sections of the village, but everyone moves freely from one section to another.

The Brahmins, who are traditionally the highest caste group, are among the poorest in the village, for their plots of land are too small to allow them to benefit much from the Green Revolution. Religious observance is not as strong as it once was, so the Brahmins' fees for conducting rituals are dropping. In the past, the Brahmins had a virtual monopoly on literacy and, for a consideration, would read and write documents for other villagers. Now that literacy is more widespread, this source of income is drying up.

On the flat expanse of the Ganges plain, a drying crop of chili peppers carpets the ground beneath an Indian fig tree with brilliant red. The Portuguese imported chilies from South America to India in the 16th century; the peppers have since become integral to the cuisine of most regions.

5

The tribal herders, though outside the traditional caste system, own goats—a material resource that the Brahmins, for example, lack. But recently, as more land has come under the plow, the nomads have had trouble finding grazing grounds. Although better off than the Brahmins, they are not as fortunate as farmers.

The one third of the villagers who are landless have more opportunities to make a living than in the past. Some commute 25 miles by train each day to jobs in Delhi. Some run shops, which cater to several villages in the area. The village weaver is no longer in business, but the potter and blacksmith survive. The arrival of tractors, trucks and motorcycles has led to a demand for auto mechanics. One or two families are destitute; they survive on the bounty of other villagers.

All in all, Akbarpur-Barota has benefited from the thrust of modernization, but many rural communities are beleaguered. India's burgeoning cities need food for their millions and land to build on; the mushrooming factories that process raw materials consume crops and wood; strip mining has destroyed large tracts of terrain. Thus, the rural population is having to subsist on a smaller proportion of the land even as its own population grows.

One consequence of the inexorable pressure on finite resources is overcultivation. Fallow periods are being reduced, and the soil is losing its fertility. As the good land is all accounted for, villagers cultivate the marginal land and steep hill slopes; the inevitable result is soil erosion.

Pastureland is being degraded as well. In the desert sands of Rajasthan, nomads herd their cattle and camels

In the dawn mist, a Karnataka villager washes the grime of the previous day's toil off his ox. Prized by all who can afford them, oxen provide power for plowing and rural transportation, as well as dung for fertilizer and fuel.

over long distances in an ever more desperate quest for a few blades of grass. In 1951, only 30 percent of the arid countryside bore crops. By the late 1980s, more than 60 percent was being cultivated at one time—the result of irrigation—at the cost of grazing lands and long fallow periods.

One of the most dangerous consequences of the pressure on land is the rapid disappearance of the forests. Trees started to vanish at an alarming rate early in this century, with the need for logs to make railroad ties and to build ships. This deforestation continued after Independence as farmers extended their plots and industry's timber needs grew. Between the early 1950s and the early 1970s, India lost 8.4 million acres of forest. By the 1980s, the forest cover was reckoned to be about 10 percent; whereas it had been 20 percent in the 1970s.

As trees become more scarce, the villagers' search for firewood becomes a major chore. Moreover, without tree cover, precious topsoil is eroded, especially on steep slopes. Erosion caused by commercial logging on the lower slopes of the Himalayas has led to flash floods and the silting of rivers. One of the worst such disasters was the Alaknanda flood in Uttar Pradesh, which took place during the 1970 monsoon. Within two hours, a 200-foot wall of water carried away entire Himalayan villages, cattle, roads, bridges and busloads of people. The silt deposits were so enormous that the irrigation system of western Uttar Pradesh was drastically affected, and crop production fell by one third that year.

As pressures on the forests mount, ecologically sensible, traditional patterns of land use are lost. Many of the tribal peoples of northeastern India have practiced slash-and-burn cultivation for centuries. They cut down mountain forests to expose irregular patches of land. In contrast to modern logging practice, they leave tree stumps and roots untouched, so that the vegetation regenerates quickly. The slashed vegetation is burned, adding mineral nutrients to the soil. A mixture of crops is often sown, and each is harvested in turn as it matures. In the past, nomadic tribes moved from plot to plot so that the poor mountain soil had time to recoup. The cycles used to take 30 to 40 years. But now, as urban and industrial pressures have restricted the extent of forest that the nomads can range over, the rotations are down to five years in many places. In such circumstances, slash-and-burn agriculture can seriously degrade the land. In most states, except Arunachal Pradesh where the population is very low, shifting cultivation has now been banned.

The challenge facing India is to make the land more productive in order to ease the pressure on resources. There is room for improvement. Scientists have calculated that India produces only about 10 percent of the grain that the land could theoretically yield, whereas many advanced countries produce about 30 percent of the theoretical maximum. Wheat is India's biggest success story, but those yields are low by world standards, thanks to uneven technological progress and incomplete land reform.

By the year 2000, roughly half the country's total arable land—1.7 billion acres—will be irrigated. That still leaves millions of farmers who will be dependent on rainfall. Acknowledging this fact, India is shifting its agricultural strategy, from the earlier focus on selected areas and miracle crops to an attempt to help the individual subsistence farmer in cultivating a rain-fed field. Current research is directed toward developing drought-resistant crops to help farmers who lack any form of irrigation.

Small farmers must also be encouraged to grow food that will give them a sound diet. The farmers' traditional mix of crops, which included several grains and beans, provided a good balance. Nowadays, wheat sown as a cash crop is replacing beans and coarse grains, such as millet; the income the

On the forest-clad slopes of the Western Ghats, a thatch-roofed dwelling stands near fields cleared for planting. This mountainous area in the south of India yields tropical crops — such as coffee, cardamom and pepper.

On the shore of the Indian Ocean in Kerala, village fishermen prepare to haul in their net, which is guided by a single man standing in chest-deep water. India's 3,500-mile-long coastline yields an abundance of fish and shellfish, which provide a valuable element in the diet of seaboard dwellers.

wheat provides is often spent on clothes and other consumer goods, rather than on nutritious food. Government subsidies for growing other crops might provide the incentive for farmers to switch back to mixed farming.

Virtually all rural people will benefit from a wise policy for forest conservation. Some of them have already taken matters into their own hands. In 1974, Himalayan villagers from the Alaknanda Valley organized themselves to protest nonviolently against commercial logging, which, by causing erosion and flooding, was jeopardizing the very existence of their villages and fields. Their strategy was simple: They threatened to hug the trees and not to detach themselves until the loggers left. The threat was rarely, if at all, carried out, but their campaign, known as the Chipko movement *(chipko* means "to hug"), attracted worldwide publicity and inspired a government review of India's forest policy. In the area where the movement originated, the villagers have undertaken extensive reforestation programs on their own land and common village tracts. The villagers' policy is: "If you cut one oak tree, plant at least three others."

The pressure on resources could be substantially eased by the rehabilitation of India's wastelands. Eroded land no longer suitable for crops may sustain trees, and some planting projects are under way. Some of the land will sustain crops if rain water is stored and its release controlled, so that it does not scour the land of nutrients.

Any program for improving the land must take into account the full gamut of villagers' activities, and the way in which different aspects of their lives are interwoven. A natural mixed forest, for example, provides not just wood for fuel but timber for farm implements, leaf humus for fertilizer, certain seeds for oil and herbs for homemade medicines. Reforestation projects that surround a village with only one type of tree, such as pine or eucalyptus, may adversely affect the very people who are supposed to benefit from them.

All too frequently, well-intentioned schemes founder because they treat different aspects of village life in isolation. In Mewat, a relatively underdeveloped pocket of the prosperous state of Haryana, Muslim village girls do not attend the village school although primary education is free. Their absence is only partly due to traditional culture, which attaches little importance to female education. It is also because, in this semiarid area, the girls have to forage for greenery to feed the cattle. The best time of the day for gathering fodder is the morning, which happens to be when school meets. Green fodder and female literacy, apparently unrelated aspects of life, are intimately connected in the Mewat villages.

National programs tend to set general priorities for development, but India's 500,000 villages cannot and will not all change at the same time and in the same way. India is too vast and diverse for that. The effectiveness of some grass-roots organizations, such as Chipko, does not mean that they have the key to the solution on a national scale. Outsiders tend either to romanticize the villagers' role in effecting change, or to ignore the villagers' point of view altogether. The villagers need help from the outside world in the shape of effective technology, adequate funds, good administration and ample information. But if the resources are to be well used, the villagers themselves must set the priorities. □

PASTORAL PACE OF A VILLAGE IN RAJASTHAN

Photographs by Pablo Bartholomew

Like country dwellers all over India, the 4,000 villagers of Harmara on the semiarid Rajasthan steppe live by the daily rhythms of field work and household labor. Families of some 50 different castes tend their animals and till their fields, mostly scattered plots totaling about five acres. Married sons build their houses next to their parents' homes, creating extended families to work each land holding. The richest farmers ease their work with machinery and by hiring the landless poor — usually at wages well below the legal minimum.

A little wealthier than the average Indian village, Harmara boasts many of the trappings of modernity — a health clinic, police station, elementary school, post office and even a telephone exchange to service the handful of families with telephones. Yet sheer survival is still the villagers' daily preoccupation. At the end of a tiring day, the men meet in the street or courtyards to share a hookah and play cards; the women gather to chat among themselves.

Assistants to a village grain merchant weigh a sack of newly harvested wheat, Harmara's principal crop. The merchant, who is also a moneylender, will deduct any outstanding loans from his payment to the farmer.

Early in the morning in Harmara's shop-lined main square, a villager walks his bicycle across one of the narrow ditches that carry runoff water from the local wells. The power lines overhead bring electricity to the community for about eight hours a day.

Oxen are foddered in a family's enclosed feed lot, while some calves and a water buffalo wait their turn in an outer pen partly fenced with thorn bushes. Many farmers in Harmara still use animal power for plowing, threshing and drawing water.

Wearing the vivid turbans distinctive to Rajasthan, village men reclaim empty milk cans from the government dairy cooperative's truck. On its daily tour to collect milk for processing at the central dairy, the truck may also pick up a load of passengers.

Men and women feed wheat into a threshing machine on land owned by one of Harmara's more prosperous farmers. The wheat harvest is in April, just before the monsoon season. When the rains come, the fields will be replanted with corn and millet, as well as peanuts and other legumes.

आजके बच्चेकलभावी

In one of the three classrooms in the village primary school, pupils study beneath a wall slogan reminding them that "Today's children will be tomorrow's citizens." About 50 percent of Harmara's children attend school; the rest cannot be spared from chores.

On the outskirts of the village, a woman unfurls a freshly washed sari in the breeze; the sun's searing heat will dry the cloth in minutes. The sari is worn only by certain castes in Rajasthan; this woman, like many in Harmara, wears an ankle-length skirt and a long shawl draped over her head.

From a dough made of wheat flour and milk, a woman shapes roti — small rounds of unleavened bread that are a staple of the north Indian diet. Her wrists are heavy with bracelets, the most valuable of which will be passed down from mother to daughter.

In preparation for a wedding, three sisters paint a design of latticework and flowers around their door. The most popular time to marry is after the monsoon, between September and November. In that period, as many as a dozen couples might wed in Harmara on one astrologically propitious day.

While early-morning traffic rumbles past, some of Calcutta's hundreds of thousands of street dwellers lie sleeping on blankets and burlap. Most are migrants from surrounding villages who have come to Calcutta in search of work and cannot find even basic accommodations in the crowded city.

CITIES OF HOPE AND STRUGGLE

The traffic in an Indian city gives the impression of a time warp. People in flowing, traditional garb mingle with businessmen in well-cut suits and pretty college students in jeans, their hair loose. Half-naked men push wheelbarrows loaded with grain bags, or ice wrapped in gunny sacks, or bedframes. Carts drawn by buffalos rumble slowly through the streets; the drivers twist the animals' tails to make them go faster, but the buffalos ignore this indignity and move at their own pace. Dilapidated carriages pulled by thin horses weave their way between modern cars, buses and incessantly tooting taxis. Cows seem to be everywhere, wandering at will along the main streets as well as the alleys.

Bicycles, usually with more than one person aboard, add to the confusion; richer men dash around on scooters, their wives perilously balanced sidesaddle on the back. Old-fashioned trucks, painted with peacocks and flowers and often with the unnecessary exhortation "Horn please!" on the rear, take their place too. To the Western visitor, the effect is one of chaos, and the chances of moving in any direction without calamity seem negligible.

Contributing to the disorder is a difference of views as to the purpose of a street. In cities that are the product of a Western consciousness, thoroughfares generally lead somewhere. But this concept of roads as arteries is at odds with the traditional Indian view of a city's function. A few wide arteries, constructed in the 19th and 20th centuries, crisscross the major cities—but the area bounded by these streets is usually a network of smaller streets and byways, many of which lead only to other back streets. A road in such a district is not a way to somewhere: It is simply the space between one row of houses and the next, one cluster of bazaar booths and the next.

Originally, the road might have been dotted with coconut palms and strips of small-scale cultivation; today it is paved and is shared chaotically and equally by motor vehicles, handcarts, bicycles, pedestrians and wandering livestock, but its character remains that of a local open space. Little wonder that people from small Indian towns and villages, who continually arrive in the larger cities in search of work, attempt to use the city streets as places to live. From their point of view, the streets are simply obvious sites on which to set up camp.

Their presence makes for some striking contrasts. Advertising billboards and the posters plastered on walls reflect the wealth and sophistication to be found at the higher levels of Indian society. They carry messages about cars, packaged foods, movies. They entreat the citizens to limit their families to "two or three" and piously urge people: "Make a friend of your income tax inspector—trust and confide in him." But sheltering beneath the legs of the billboards is likely to be a little colony of

6

Three dhoti-clad men perform yoga exercises on Calcutta's maidan — the largest park in the city. Behind them looms the Victoria Memorial, built between 1906 and 1921 to house mementos of British colonial India.

squatters, living their marginal existence in huts that are roofed with whatever scraps come to hand.

Staking their claim to a meager stretch of open space, the squatters contribute to the mind-boggling overcrowding of India's cities. London has 10,400 people to the square mile and New York 26,000—but Calcutta counts more than 98,000 and Bombay a staggering 114,400. Though more acute today than ever before, crowding has always been a feature of Indian cities, at least in the north and center. Many of these cities were once walled for defense; houses were built several stories high, huddled close together within the protective confines. Often the walls still stand, and it is only recently that housing has spread beyond the old city limits. In the south, however, such cities as Mysore and Trivandrum were built without walls and have a more spacious aspect. Many of their ornate, red-tiled dwellings are one story.

Whatever their layout, Indian cities have always been humming centers of commerce. Vendors of goods and services are everywhere, and trading is active. With storage space in the home at a premium, and refrigerators all too liable to be inactivated by power cuts, most families ordinarily buy perishable foods fresh for each meal. They bargain for each item as a matter of course, but they do so courteously, without becoming heated.

In the heart of a venerable city such as Old Delhi, one bazaar begins almost where the previous one ends. Each has its speciality—paper, silver, plastic household goods. The spice bazaars are the most colorful, with their glowing mounds of turmeric, saffron and chilies. The fruit bazaars offer seasonal produce in profusion: Piles of mangoes appear in May, oranges in the winter. The ground floors of the tall bazaar houses are subdivided to provide a number of traders with booths, which often serve as workshops and family homes as well. Some traders operate from mere alcoves that are set into buildings a little above ground level. They sit cross-legged, surrounded by their wares. Freestanding stalls fill much of the area between the houses, offering coconuts, shoeshines, glasses of cold water or typing services.

The newcomer to India is most struck by such indigenous features of Indian cities as the milling street life and the ubiquitous bazaars. Yet the influence of the West is profound. All the old cities have been affected by Western culture, and some have been transformed. The British-founded cities, except New Delhi, assumed an Indian character almost from their inception, but their architecture is a powerful reminder of their European origins.

An example of the 20th-century transformation of a historic Indian city is Bangalore, in Karnataka. Founded in the early 16th century by a petty chieftain named Kempe Gowda, it has in the last two decades acquired much in common with any booming city elsewhere in the world. It is rightly described in the tourist brochures as the "city of gardens," one of the loveliest of which was laid out by an 18th-century ruler. But it is also today the city of India's aeronautics and electronics industries. Bangalore is one of the world's 10 fastest-growing cities and has now reached fifth place in India (behind Calcutta, Bombay, Delhi and Madras). High-rises are pushing up between its spacious bungalows.

The beautiful old provincial center of Jodhpur, in the Rajasthan desert, is a much less frenetic place. The Maharaja still lives in his grand, mock-Mogul, 20th-century palace (part of which is now a hotel) and interests himself in public affairs. A fort begun in the 14th century dominates the town from a cliff-top location; in its shade lie the flat-topped blue houses of a substantial Brahmin colony. Jodhpur is a highly traditional city, and one whole colony of Brahmins here devote themselves entirely to the casting of horoscopes. The city is also celebrated as a center for Indian music. Certain castes make their living from performing: The gentle and plangent sounds of sitars come from many streets and alleys as you walk past them. Motor vehicles are rare in the middle of town: Camel carts and bicycles occupy the streets.

Yet Jodhpur is no backwater or carefully preserved museum. Its population of more than 400,000 has spread far beyond the old city walls; it is a railhead and a service center for a wide area, and it has an atmosphere of quiet prosperity. Jodhpur has very little significant industry, but outside the walls lie an important university, an air-force base, and a government-sponsored organization that is investigating solar and wind power and the agricultural possibilities of the desert.

In Madras, Bombay and Calcutta, the three great cities that were semiautonomous seats of government under British rule, Western influences are much more intricately woven into the fabric. The three cities were established in the late 17th century as defensible colonial trading posts—Bombay by the Portuguese, Calcutta and Madras by the British. A generation or two later, each consisted of a fort or stronghold surrounded by an area cleared as a field

of fire. Today, this zone has become the town *maidan*, or open green space—an invaluable asset that eases the oppression of overcrowding.

Madras, conveniently situated for ships that had made the long voyage east around the southern tip of Africa, grew large before the other two. By the late 18th century, the city had already achieved much of the extent and shape it retains today. The layout of the middle of the city is a classic gridiron pattern like that of a New World city, with the spaciousness typical of southern India. In the 19th century, lacking the raw materials to become a major manufacturing center, it stagnated economically, while Calcutta and Bombay both grew enormously in size and importance. Today, engineering and vehicle plants are multiplying to supplement Madras' traditional industry, weaving. Slums have appeared too, but they are not India's worst: Southern Indians are generally more fastidious in their social habits than northerners, and they manage to impose order on the worst accommodations. Much of Madras retains an attractive, old-fashioned air; its tree-lined residential streets, though scruffy, have hardly changed.

Calcutta's heyday was in the 18th and 19th centuries, when the Far East was opened up. Its residential districts resemble the parts of London designed at the same period—low-rise dwellings arranged in graceful squares and crescents. The city's paper factories and jute warehouses, constructed of brick, might almost have been imported wholesale from one of Britain's northern industrial cities in the 19th century. Until 1912, Calcutta was the imperial capital, though its location on the oozing black mud of the Hooghly delta was widely held to be unsuitable for a market town, let alone a world capital. Mark Twain, there on a lecture tour in the 1890s, said that the climate was enough to turn a brass doorknob mushy.

Calcutta entered a long decline when

6

the Suez Canal was opened in 1869, and the city found itself no longer on the main trade routes. Today it has become a synonym for urban squalor and decay. Its stucco townhouses are in such appalling disrepair that a number of them collapse in every cyclone and monsoon downpour. Labor disputes are rife in its factories. Power cuts are a daily occurrence, the traffic is a nightmare, and the misery of the destitute is visible on every street.

Yet Calcutta also has a well-earned reputation as India's most intellectually lively city. Since the 19th century, Western ideas have fused with indigenous culture in a uniquely fruitful way. Calcutta University is the largest in the world. Publishing houses based in Calcutta outnumber those in all the rest of India, and the city is home to more than 700 literary magazines. Literary circles and amateur dramatic groups abound, and although Calcutta's film industry is small, some of its output—the most notable being that of director Satyajit Ray—is world-renowned.

Bombay was founded on the other side of the subcontinent on a cluster of seven islands, but subsequent land reclamation turned them into one. It came into its own as a port and manufacturing center with the coming of steamships in the 1830s, followed by the opening of the Suez Canal a generation later; its rise mirrored Calcutta's decline. As its stature increased, the city's apologists began suggesting loudly that it was surely Bombay's glorious destiny to house the imperial establishment. In the 1870s and 1880s, a grand chain of Saracenic-Gothic building was constructed with that intention along Bombay's *maidans*, facing the Arabian Sea. But Bombay never became the capital, and the pinnacled edifices have lost their ocean frontage to land reclamation. Yet the city has continued to prosper and has long spread beyond the island to the mainland.

A prostitute solicits customers from the doorway of a brothel in Bombay's red-light district. Some 20,000 prostitutes serve the hundreds of thousands of men who have migrated alone in search of work, leaving their wives in their home villages.

Today, Bombay houses an enormous film industry, manufactures everything from bicycles to pharmaceuticals and serves as India's finance center. Superficially, Bombay is the most Westernized city on the subcontinent. British visitors at once feel at home with its red double-decker buses and its large Victorian buildings. American tourists, sighting its newer, high-rise buildings from the ocean, might almost believe that they are approaching New York or San Francisco.

Delhi, the city that did succeed Calcutta as capital, is the only major center in India where Western and Eastern elements have failed to merge. Old Delhi, the northern side of town, is centuries old. The massive Red Fort, built by the Mogul emperor Shah Jahan in the 17th century, dominates the skyline, and the main street is the silver bazaar. Old Delhi is typical of historic Indian cities in its colorful overcrowding; nowadays, however, polluted and tourist-conscious, it is less pleasant than many of the self-contained provincial cities it resembles.

When people speak of Delhi today, they usually mean New Delhi, a 20th-century creation built alongside the old city but kept separate. There was a modest European presence in Delhi during the 19th century, but when the British eventually planned New Delhi, they saw it as a public-relations exercise. Because Delhi had long been a Mogul capital and center of indigenous power, it seemed fitting that the new imperial capital should be established there. And when the British left in 1947, it was deemed essential that the new all-Indian government should move into their buildings.

The great public buildings and official residences were designed by the British architect Sir Edwin Lutyens, in an entirely Western style more reminiscent of Washington, D.C., than of anywhere else. New Delhi is conceived in a spread-out, garden-suburb idiom that presents problems in the arid months of the hot season: A great deal of money is spent on watering and tending the expanses of public parks to keep them in existence. But the neoclassical buildings are lovely on a clear winter morning as the mist is lifting, and in the side roads, splendid bungalows—one-story houses, often with verandas—occupy secluded gardens.

New Delhi is overwhelmingly a city for the wealthy and Westernized. Its society is composed largely of ambitious politicians and civil servants. The bazaars are missing, and the poor do not mingle with the rich as they do in other Indian towns.

Right from their inception, the im-

A car pushes its way through a crush of cyclists, rickshaws and handcarts in a street in Old Delhi. Here, as in every Indian city, traffic regulations are blithely ignored: Vehicles speed through red lights, pass on the wrong side and constantly switch lanes to avoid ambling cows.

perial cities of Bombay, Calcutta and Madras offered countless niches for Indians of every class. Most of the British people who lived there were in administration or business. Except for the substantial army of British soldiers and their families, working-class British people did not come to India. Thus, in creating their great trading metropolises, the British created opportunities for Indian artisans and entrepreneurs as much as for themselves. Indian talent and enterprise flooded into the big cities in the 19th century; Indians built many of the houses, the bazaars, the workshops, the mosques and the water tanks. The flood has never abated. By 1981, Bombay was reckoned to have eight million people, Calcutta nine, and Madras four, but these can be only rough estimates when the total is mounting by hundreds daily.

People flock to the big cities because they offer so many opportunities—opportunities for work, for advancement, for life itself. Many come because they can look forward to little or nothing in their villages of origin, whereas the city, however intimidating, however chaotic, squalid and overcrowded, does present innumerable possibilities for keeping body and soul together, perhaps even for making good.

Overcrowding, indeed, is a sign of the cities' vitality. A similar phenomenon occurred in the major British, German and American cities during the Industrial Revolution in the 19th century. What Westerners are seeing in Calcutta and Bombay is their own past—capital enterprise in the raw, from the rich speculator cramming high-rises onto land previously occupied by bungalows and trees to the ex-villager who has set up a tea or cigarette

Blue and white houses cluster around the base of the rocky eminence that dominates Jodhpur, once the capital of a princely state in the Rajasthan desert. Blue houses belong to Brahmins; the custom of one caste distinguishing its homes by color is unique to Jodhpur.

stall or shoe-repair booth on a few feet of pavement in one of the most overcrowded places in the world. Certainly, India's urban slums provide living conditions as squalid and minimal as anywhere else on earth. But they have rightly been called "slums of hope."

Moreover, it is important to discriminate between degrees of poverty. Some slums look like agglomerations of blackened chicken coops, perched illegally on any vacant scrap of land, near dangerous railroad tracks or, most often, alongside the waters of some stinking creek, which is made far worse by the fact of being the sole water supply and sewer for a couple of thousand extra people. But others have been on their sites for many years and, over the course of time, have acquired a degree of legality: tiled roofs; an intricate social organization, including shops and workshops; and finally municipal services in the form of standpipes, latrines and sometimes even streetlights. Life in such a place, though short on comfort and space by the standards of much of the rest of the world, is not too bad in social terms, and a good deal better than starvation in a rural village.

Likewise, the people who live on the streets within the very shadow of grand hotels and banks are not always in desperate straits or destitute. There is, for instance, a family that lives in and around a tree on a pleasant street near Bombay Hospital. Their routine of life is well established and unchanging, except that the children grow; the baby hung in a cloth sling from one of the big banyan tree's branches becomes a plump toddler, to be replaced by a new occupant in the sling. The tree, large, old and half hollow, hung with little sacred icons and garlands, is not big enough to accommodate everybody—although it can comfortably take three adults sitting underneath it to enjoy a glass of tea on a wet or too-hot day. The extended family has colonized a long strip of adjacent pavement, hanging spare clothes on the hospital railings and rigging up cloth awnings under which they have set their sleeping cots.

One member, the grandfather, has an ironing business, and each day he can be seen plying an old-fashioned charcoal-heated steam iron at a rickety ironing board: The laundry workers from a nearby hotel contract work out to him, which, if the guests only knew it, would account for the fact that garments are sometimes returned with stains that they did not have when sent. One of his sons has a profitable soft-drink stall, for which the young man buys ice twice daily from the wandering iceman, and another son is a newspaper vendor who pitches his wares farther up the street.

The three women of the tree house come and go; they have occasional cleaning jobs in the hospital and in nearby apartment houses. But when they are at home, they are constantly busy, like dutiful Indian wives from all walks of life, washing their clothes or their children or the dishes, with water fetched every morning at dawn in great brass jars from a local standpipe. In the early morning, and again when darkness falls, they cook meals of rice and carefully spiced vegetables on a tiny alcohol-burning stove; the family all gathers around and eats from a single dish. The children are adequately dressed and do not beg, and the eldest boy likes to sit reading. The small ones are firmly admonished to go and relieve themselves farther down the street, in the gutter near an untenanted bit of sidewalk: The bigger ones and the adults, following Hindu custom, steal out onto the nearby *maidan* under cover of dark.

With virtually no material needs other than food and clothing, the family maintains itself through its various small enterprises. Many street dwellers in similar circumstances even manage to save enough money to keep an elderly parent in the home village.

Such people are the elite of street dwellers. The Muslim families who camp about 200 yards from the tree house—and earn their living as cobblers and vendors—are dirtier and poorer. In this they are not atypical of their coreligionists. Muslims are found at all levels of Indian society, but since Independence, when many middle-class Muslims emigrated to Pakistan, those of their faith who remained behind have made up a disproportionate fraction of India's destitute.

The luckier ones on the street near Bombay hospital sell flowers—which they have purchased at dawn from a large market in uptown Bombay—to

Muslim women take a stroll on a winter afternoon in Srinagar, capital of Kashmir. The tall houses that line the street are made of stone bonded with timber — a building technique typical of the Himalayan region.

the worshippers at a nearby mosque. They sit all day by their baskets of petals, threading and braiding; here, a refreshing, delicate aura of scent and moisture cuts across the Indian street smells of dust, gas fumes, burning charcoal, spices and a persistent odor of urine. The Muslim flower sellers do a thriving trade: Even very poor people will spend money for a perishable flower garland to wear in their hair, just as they will be precise about what they want in their *pan*—an individually concocted portion of leaf-wrapped betel nut and lime, which they will chew on throughout the day.

There are people living still farther up the street, where the relatively prosperous street camps give way to the trash dumps at the back entrance of the huge main train station, Victoria Terminus. Here, goats are kept on the trash piles, and both children and adults beg as a matter of course. They are probably the main customers for the illicit liquor that is brewed nightly in a derelict British graveyard nearby. Religious orthodoxy constrains many Indians from touching alcohol, but some of the street people in Bombay, as in many Western cities, are alcoholics.

While the poorest of the poor truly have no choice but to sleep on the street, many of the younger men who bed down every night on the sidewalks of India's big cities, either on cots or simply on pieces of cloth, are dressed in clothes that are clearly not beggars' rags. These street people have homes to go to and relatives who cook and wash for them. But in most cases, these homes would be the one-room tenements where more than 70 percent of Calcutta's and Bombay's citizens live, often shared with a collection of relatives. Small wonder that, except during the monsoon, the younger and freer members of the family prefer the space and airiness of the nighttime street.

At any hour of the day, there are vastly more people on the streets—mostly men—just walking or standing around, than strictly speaking need to be there. In many households that are

ENTERTAINERS WHO ROAM THE STREETS

Snake charmers, sword swallowers, jugglers and puppeteers are everyday sights on the streets of Indian cities. Men dressed as monkeys scamper into shops, acrobats leap through blazing hoops, storytellers recount ancient epics. The performers belong to many castes — all of them low in the hierarchy; each caste has its own speciality, which is handed down from generation to generation.

The street virtuosos' ancestors were rural itinerants who wandered from one village to another, performing and passing on news. But in some villages, traditions have been weakened by communal television sets, making the lives of such entertainers more difficult. Many have moved to distant cities and rarely return to the region of their roots.

Even in the cities, the performers struggle to survive. In several metropolises, any street act that can be seen as begging is illegal, and the artists must be always on the move to evade the police. Many have no home, but live on the sidewalks or in surburban tent cities. One such slum on the edge of Delhi has become a colony of 3,000 performers of every description. Acknowledging their joint problems and aspirations, they have surmounted caste differences and banded together as the Cooperative of Forgotten and Neglected Artists. Officially recognized, they practice their craft without police harassment.

An ecstatic young performer on the tambourine joins forces with a string player and a drummer to divert passersby on a Delhi street. The musicians are members of a cooperative of folk artists in Shadipur, a West Delhi slum.

A snake charmer, carrying his cobra in an open basket, roams a Calcutta market in search of a suitable spot to entertain the crowds. In the wild, cobras are extremely venomous, but snake charmers usually render them harmless by removing the fangs.

6

not wealthy, it is the custom for the male members of the family to absent themselves for most of the day, whether at work or not, in order to get out of each other's way and give the women some privacy. The sight of men on the street, clad only in loincloths or old shorts and giving themselves an energetic shower with water from a standpipe, is a common one; women, if they have a home or shelter, are more likely to wash indoors.

Movie theaters offer another welcome escape from cramped quarters, and Indian city dwellers are avid moviegoers. Teenagers will line up to see a film several times a month, even if the program has not changed. Married couples often follow suit, in search of a little respite from family pressures. The one-room apartment that is home for so many may be in a high-rise in the center of town, in a two-story building erected near factory gates in the late 19th century, in a modern cement building on the road to the airport, in a dilapidated old villa that has been divided and subdivided, or in rows of one-story dwellings provided by the government and known as hutments.

The accommodations may be relatively spacious, or a dark closet barely 10 feet square; its door may open straight onto an alleyway or a high landing, but the basic form is the same. Nearly always it has an adjoining open-air, semicovered balcony or veranda, where the cooking is done, and in the better-equipped apartments, there may also be an individual shower, perhaps even a toilet. A visit to such a comparatively comfortable home is revealing. Here live people who are worlds away from the street dwellers: shop owners, skilled workers, drivers, government employees, journalists, teachers, even doctors. The men emerge each morning with shirts freshly ironed, the children go to school in tidy white uniforms, the women wear bright saris and jewelry on holidays and for other special occasions.

Yet these people are keeping up standards in quarters so confined as to ap-

Caught by the floodwaters of the Ganges during the monsoon, citizens of Varanasi wade about their business with a resigned composure. The annual inundation forces many shops to close and sends thousands of the city's street dwellers back to their villages of origin to help in the fields.

Low, stone-walled huts roofed with lengths of tarpaulin serve as homes for thousands in a Delhi slum. Most such communities lack clean drinking water, electricity or sewage facilities.

pall their equivalents in Europe and North America. Crammed into one room will be several couches or divans on which the entire family must somehow arrange themselves at night (at least during the monsoon season), a display of decorated cushions, and a cupboard bursting with clothes and staple foods and invariably kept locked. There will almost certainly be a refrigerator and a fan.

Nearly always there will be a glass-fronted cabinet with the best teacups arranged on top and, along the shelves, maybe a few books and ornaments—Kashmiri boxes brought back from a wedding journey to the north, a miniature Taj Mahal from a trip to Agra. Quite likely, too, there will be some souvenirs from England, Canada or the Arabian Gulf, testament to relatives who have gone to seek their fortune in some faraway place and have perhaps stayed there, coming back occasionally to dazzle the family with tales of foreign money or welfare benefits, or to comfort them in their stay-at-home role with stories about cold, loneliness and racial prejudice.

These middle-class families—for they would unhesitatingly style themselves so—living as many as 10 to a room, would of course obtain prettier and more spacious housing for far less money in a small town or village. But how would they live there? How could they hope to educate their children for better things? They are glad to accept such exiguous, and expensive, quarters in one of the great cities for the same reason that the poorest people accept far less—because there are multiple job opportunities and hope for the future in the cities.

Such is the demand for living space in the cities that a newcomer has virtually no immediate hope of finding a private room. Rentals are passed on within a family and never come on the open market. The situation causes immense difficulties for the enterprising young man, probably a graduate, who has achieved some sought-after white-collar job in the city but has no relatives

On a Calcutta street, some of the residents of a nearby apartment building rinse off in water welling up from a broken pipe through the cracked sidewalk. Beyond, others gather around a hand pump. Most tenements do not have running water, and many occupants resort to bathing outdoors.

there with whom he can live. He may have to keep up appearances while camping on the streets or bedding down in his place of work or in the room of a friend.

City life at this middle level can be a more complex battle than at the levels of outright poverty. The laundry worker, the fruit seller, the rickshaw boy, the ragpicker may live from hand to mouth, laboring long hours for a few rupees a day, but they have no appearances to maintain: They do not need to impress anyone, not even prospective wives. When such men marry, they pick someone of their own kind, often very young, accustomed to hard work, someone who has never encountered privacy in her life and who will settle down without complaint in whatever slum can be found.

A clerk, however, courting a girl from a family of moderate means, has a real problem. He wants her—and the dowry her father can provide. His own family approves. Time is passing; he wants children and the status that marriage brings. But there may be absolutely nowhere within his means that he can take his bride but the one-room family home, already the domicile of seven or eight people. For a week or two after the wedding, the whole clan will tactfully take themselves off to the courtyard or up onto the flat roof for the night, but they cannot be expected to do this forever. And when another child arrives, the one-room apartment will be no bigger.

Young couples at this level of society have probably never been alone together before their wedding night. But at a slightly higher social level, families that consider themselves modern will permit engaged couples to make decorous excursions to the movies together. Shyly getting acquainted with each other before their arranged marriage takes place, they hold hands in the air-conditioned darkness.

The parents of such couples exude a pleased air of cosmopolitanism, and send their children to schools that follow British models. They reject what they consider old-fashioned prejudices. They allow their daughters to play tennis in white shorts, for example, exposing an area of flesh that traditional families would consider unseemly. The father relishes his glass of whiskey, ignoring religious prohibitions. The mother plays bridge in the club where the British used to congregate. Some members of this stratum of urban Indians have even taken the bold step of rejecting the idea of living with their extended family, in favor of the nuclear one. Yet underneath they tend to be family-oriented; their life revolves around matrimonial ties and business deals (often intermingled), with extravagant weddings as the linchpins of social obligation.

There is also real wealth in the Indian cities—especially in Bombay, which has for several decades been the most financially buoyant; in Calcutta, too, in spite of its problems; in Delhi, of course; and increasingly in Madras, Bangalore and other growing centers. The number of well-to-do professional and business people has risen steeply since the late 1970s. The magazines they read, such as *India Today* and *Sunday,* are filled with glossy advertisements for saris, suits, air conditioners and hotels. Some of the new wealth has trickled down the social scale, but discrepancies remain enormous in India.

In Bombay, the newly rich tend to live in high-rise apartments that display Manhattan-style glamor. In Calcutta

6

On the grassy rooftop terrace of a 19-story apartment building in Bombay's exclusive Malabar Hill district, three residents enjoy tea and sweets set out by a servant. Their view encompasses the Arabian Sea and the modern high-rise buildings of central Bombay.

and Delhi, they are more likely to be found in many-roomed bungalows with a staff of servants (who have their quarters at the back), surrounded by lawns on which sprinklers play. Some of the bungalows, inherited from British days, lie very close to city centers. But spacious accommodations in prime locations are becoming increasingly rare, and most of the bungalow developments built after Independence are four or five miles from city centers.

These flat-roofed residences are built in a variety of imported styles—elaborate iron grillwork features on some, Arabian domes and arches on others. Marble is used in abundance. The houses are usually serviced by a small shopping center, where the servants buy food and take the laundry to be washed. To an outsider who wanders into an affluent colony, the servants are far more visible than their masters. Since they all have cars, the owners of the houses are seen on the streets only when they take their early-morning walk with the dog.

Fear of crime is prevalent: Most families station a servant permanently beside the high gate that leads into their property, and groups of families join together to pay a night watchman who will patrol the area, tapping the ground with his night stick to warn burglars away.

In more traditional circles, however, the rich in India have not gone in for luxury homes. The older wealthy families tend to disguise their prosperity, living in quite shabby buildings in city centers. Many of them invest their fortunes in land or jewelry and have surprisingly modest lifestyles. If they do spend freely, it is on family pleasures: They eat extremely well, they entertain lavishly in hotels and they have taken to video with unbridled enthusiasm. Weddings are the ultimate family occasion, and, notwithstanding legislation that places an upper limit on wedding expenditure, rich families will spend a fortune receiving hundreds of guests in the grandest possible style.

Not enough of their wealth reaches the coffers of the municipalities. Large Indian cities, financed jointly by the state governments and their own property taxes, are chronically short of money. Central government sometimes bails them out in a crisis, and the World Bank, recognizing Calcutta's uniquely acute problems, has in recent years made massive loans to the city. However, efficient use of the resources is hampered by infighting among politicians and by widespread corruption. Of the many pressing problems the municipal governments face, the most acute are the unsnarling of transportation, the provision of clean drinking water and the disposal of sewage.

The teeming and diverse life on the streets is the root cause of the transportation chaos. But the problem is exacerbated by the sheer size of the largest cities and the old-style, labor-intensive way in which most businesses and factories are run. Industry, still very often located in the city centers, causes a good deal of heavy commercial traffic through crowded streets. The cities' innumerable offices, large and small, generate a twice-daily tide of commuters from distant residential suburbs. The packed buses, trolleys and commuter trains of India's largest cities are one of the sights of the world: People literally hang onto the outside while the vehicles move at full speed. Not infrequently, individuals fall, particularly from the open doors of moving trains, losing arms, legs or life itself beneath the wheels.

Each city tries to deal with its long-standing traffic crisis in its own way. Bombay has banned games of cricket, still common in the middle of downtown intersections a few years back, and has excluded the unstable and undisciplined motorcycle rickshaws from the city center. They still circulate, however, in Bombay's endless uptown suburbs. No solution has yet been found to

A Sikh boy battles against electronic aliens in a Calcutta video arcade. Although he wears a European jacket, his hair — following Sikh custom — remains uncut, bound into a topknot and covered with a turban.

the problems of the monsoon season. In the low-lying central part of the city—the area reclaimed from a salt marsh—cars and motorcycles, trucks and buses cannot navigate the flooded streets; and for a few weeks, horse-drawn traffic comes into its own again.

Calcutta, unlike other cities, has kept its old trolleys, which run down the middle of the road and block other traffic. To ease the horrendous congestion in the city, Calcutta has inaugurated an underground rail line—the first in southern Asia—although the marshy ground on which the city is built is far from ideal for such a venture. The foundation stone was laid in 1972, but a series of financial crises and technical hitches delayed the opening until 1984. In June of that year, just when part of the track was ready for a trial run, monsoon rain flooded the system and damaged subway cars and cables. By October, repairs were complete and the entrances had been built up above ground level to prevent a recurrence of the inundation. Trains now run smoothly on part of the system; officials promise that the entire 10-mile line will be completed by the end of the 1980s, but Calcuttans are skeptical. Meanwhile, the estimated cost of the enterprise has escalated more than five times, and ironically, the surface traffic has become even more chaotic as a result of excavating the tunnel.

In the short term, there is little hope of solving the traffic crisis of India's cities. But there are signs that, as has happened in the West, industry will gradually retreat from the choked hearts of Calcutta and Bombay to developments on the periphery of the cities, and indeed to other areas, such as Bangalore. The dispersion of industry will ease the pressure on the most beleaguered places.

The provision of clean water and sewage disposal has been a perpetual saga in India's major cities. There was a brief and happy period in the late

In the historic city of Jaipur, a photographer — one of India's millions of small-scale street traders — waits, perched in the shade of his umbrella, for customers. An associate develops the portraits on the spot to provide instant souvenirs.

19th century when Calcutta was the imperial capital and Bombay was its rival; the municipal services of both were being laid down, new water reservoirs were constructed, and for a few years both cities were statistically healthier, with a lower death rate from cholera than London. But in the 20th century, to drink unboiled or unfiltered water in a number of Indian cities is to do so at one's peril; yet the mass of the working people do, and consequently many of them die before their time.

Cholera is endemic in Calcutta and probably in Bombay also, although the issue is officially evaded; locals prefer just to talk about "gastrointestinal infections." Even if not actual cholera, such infections—which include a range of virulent dysenteries, both bacterial and amoebic—are particularly lethal to the young, who have not yet had a chance to develop any immunity. It is a common sight in Indian cities to see a troop of neatly dressed school children heading off to class, each carrying his or her own thermos of boiled water.

Calcutta's sewage problem is more obvious than Bombay's because less has been spent on Calcutta during its century of gradual decline: Many of Calcutta's citizens have no access to modern bathrooms. Bombay, however, has a concealed problem which may be just as bad. Because Bombay is on an island linked to the mainland only by narrow causeways in the north, the water and sewage pipes all have to come by the same route, usually in the same trenches. Both sets of pipes are old and leaky; in addition, shantytown residents illicitly puncture the water pipes in order to tap supplies for themselves. Given that the demand for water in any case outstrips the supply, and that many water mains are literally sucked dry at certain times of day, the perfect conditions are created for a flow of sewage into the water supply.

Citizens made ill by inadequate public-health standards in the cities will, with luck, find themselves in the care of one of the many free hospitals, subsidized clinics and other charities that care for the sick and destitute. To Westerners, the best-known charitable institution in India is the refuge for the dying in Calcutta, founded by the Albanian nun Mother Teresa. But India has a long tradition of charitable provision of its own; orphanages, shelters and food-distribution centers are numerous. By Western standards, the big public hospitals of the great cities may appear disorganized and of questionable cleanliness; but some of the medicine practiced in them is as good as anywhere in the world. The All-India Institute of Medical Sciences in Delhi, for example, has a well-earned reputation for sophisticated heart surgery.

Even when the infrastructure is functioning reasonably well, existence in Indian cities demands a complex social organization and much forbearance from everybody. Life at very high population densities, with people of so many different communities and economic levels living cheek by jowl, is potentially explosive. Not surprisingly, when the unspoken social contract breaks down in Indian cities it does so completely, with murderous riots between one community and another.

Religious differences or economic rivalries often lie behind the outbursts of mob violence, but a major contributing factor is the strain and precariousness inherent in the lives of so many Indian citizens. There were terrible riots in Calcutta in 1926 caused by religious antagonisms, exacerbated by disputes between castes and anti-British feeling. Calcutta saw even worse violence in 1946 and 1947, which lasted months, on and off, and left thousands dead. Once again, religion was the spark that ignited other resentments.

Ever since Independence, particularly in the 1960s and 1970s, when Calcutta seemed to be on the point of social collapse, a repetition of these scenes has been ominously predicted. And yet, against all expectations, Calcutta appears to be managing marginally better these days. It was prosperous Bombay, in the early 1980s, that was the scene of a prolonged and sometimes violent strike in the textile mills in the heart of the city, and then of ugly riots in the suburbs between Muslims and Hindus.

But much of the time, despite the frustrations and injustices, peace is maintained. The willingness of many of the city's residents to perform services for relatively small sums of money has much to do with this harmony, for it makes for a great deal of mutual benefit. Even families in quite modest circumstances will employ a servant to clean and wash, which means that they themselves are relieved of such troublesome chores—and are thereby freed to go and stand in lines for sugar, kerosene or railroad berths—while countless widows and teen-age boys who would otherwise be destitute find minimal employment.

The best example of mutual cooperation in a cheap-labor economy is probably the Bombay *dabbawallahs,* the men who collect and distribute the lunch boxes. Their official title is the Union of Tiffin Box Suppliers; they number thousands, so great is the demand among Bombay husbands for lunch freshly cooked by their own wives,

who indulge their individual tastes.

The traffic in Bombay is so slow that commuters must leave home before 7 o'clock. If the wives were to have the lunches prepared in time for their husbands to carry them to work, they would be obliged to start before dawn. Thanks to the *dabbawallahs,* the women can settle down to the task once they have seen their husbands off. They prepare three or four different dishes—say rice, spiced fresh vegetables, chick-peas and curds—and enclose each one in a separate compartment of an aluminium lunch box. In the middle of the morning, a *dabbawallah* arrives at the house to pick up the meal and take it by foot, bicycle or handcart to the nearest train station. When the lunches arrive at the commercial center of Bombay, the *dabbawallahs* transport them to the *maidan,* sort out the boxes themselves, and then take them to the offices where the husbands are awaiting this delivery of home cooking. The lunches are tepid by now, but that is the way Indian food is often eaten.

Most of the *dabbawallahs* are illiterate; the boxes bear not names but strange hieroglyphs. The circles, dots, slashes and swastikas, elements in the code long ago devised by the *dabbawallahs,* denote train stations, office buildings and transfer points. It is the Union's boast that no lunch box has ever been known to go astray.

The tiffin-box business represents one of the best sides of Indian life. Inventive, painstaking and efficient, the *dabbawallahs* exemplify the Indian capacity to make something of the smallest opportunity, to rise above any shortcomings in their education or circumstances. To anyone trying to read into India's future, stories such as theirs offer the assurance that, whatever is in store for them, Indians will survive, adapt and flourish. □

ACKNOWLEDGMENTS

The index for this book was prepared by Vicki Robinson. For their assistance in the preparation of this volume, the editors also wish to thank the following people and institutions: Jyoti Basu, Chief Minister, West Bengal, India; Mike Brown, London; the Chowdhary family, Calcutta; Commonwealth Institute Library, London; Una Da Cunha, Bombay; Jane Curry, London; Government of India Tourist Office, London; Helen Grubin, London; S. K. Khasnavis, Indian Engineering Export Promotion Council, London; George Michell, London; Geoffrey Moorhouse, North Yorkshire, England; Robin Olson, London; Camelia Punjabi, Taj Hotels, India; Aruna and Bunker Roy, Rajasthan, India; James Shepherd, London; Social Work and Research Center, Tilonia, Rajasthan, India; Deborah Thompson, London; Jacquey Visick, London; Western India Turf Club, Bombay, India.

PICTURE CREDITS

Credits from left to right are separated by semicolons, from top to bottom by dashes.

Cover: Henry Wilson, London. Front endpaper: Map by Roger Stewart, London. Back endpaper: Digitized map by Ralph Scott/Chapman Bounford, London.

1, 2: © Flag Research Center, Winchester, Massachusetts. 6, 7: Victor Lamont from Camerapix Hutchison Library, London. 8, 9: Raghubir Singh from The John Hillelson Agency, London; digitized image by Ralph Scott/Chapman Bounford, London. 10, 11: David Beatty, Bath, England. 12, 13: Henry Wilson from Robert Harding Picture Library, London. 14, 15: Pablo Bartholomew, Bombay. 17: Henry Wilson from Robert Harding Picture Library, London. 18: J. Henebry, Wilmette, Illinois; Mike McQueen from The Image Bank, London. 19: Terry Madison from The Image Bank, London; Sybil Sassoon from Robert Harding Picture Library, London (2). 20: Digitized map by Ralph Scott/ Chapman Bounford, London. 21: Raghubir Singh from The John Hillelson Agency, London. 22, 23: George Shelley, New York. 24, 25: Michael Freeman, London. 27: Tim Beddow from Daily Telegraph Color Library, London. 28, 29: Lyle Lawson, Virginia Water, Surrey, England. 30: Dilip Mehta from Contact Press Images/Colorific!, London. 31: Christopher Cormack from Impact Photos, London. 32, 33: Jana Koldrt, Zurich. 34, 35: Michael Freeman, London. 36, 37: Henry Wilson from Robert Harding Picture Library, London. 39: Raghubir Singh from The John Hillelson Agency, London. 40: Henry Wilson from Robert Harding Picture Library, London. 41: Pierre Toutain, Paris, 43: Baldev/SYGMA from The John Hillelson Agency, London. 44: Raghubir Singh from The John Hillelson Agency, London. 45: Jana Koldrt, Zurich. 47: David Beatty, Bath, England. 48, 49: Pablo Bartholomew, Bombay. 51: Raghubir Singh from The John Hillelson Agency, London. 52, 53: Henry Wilson from Robert Harding Picture Library, London. 54-65: J. Henebry, Wilmette, Illinois. 66, 67: Clive Friend, Cobham, Surrey, England. 69: Courtesy Sarnath Museum, Uttar Pradesh, India, photograph by Clive Friend, Cobham, Surrey, England. 70: *Shah Jahan and One of His Sons Riding in Escort* by Manohar, 1615, courtesy Victoria and Albert Museum, London, photograph by Michael Holford, Loughton, Essex, England. 71: *A Prince and His Favorite,* miniature in the style of Pahari, School of Chambra, 18th century, courtesy of Musée Guimet, Paris, photograph by Michael Holford, Loughton, Essex, England. 73: Photograph by Eileen Tweedy, London. 74, 75: *First English Trading Post, Suratte* from *Livro do Estado da India Oriental,* 1646, f.181-182, courtesy of The British Library, London. 76: *Mohenjo-Daro Dancing Girl* from National Museum, New Delhi, India, photograph by Clive Friend, Cobham, Surrey, England; Photograph by Clive Friend, Cobham, Surrey, England; *Akbar, Emperor of Hindustan* from the Department of Oriental Antiquities, courtesy of the Trustees of the British Museum, London. 77: Courtesy Victoria and Albert Museum, London, photograph by Michael Holford, Loughton, Essex, England — BBC Hulton Picture Library, London; Delhi Photos Black Star/Colorific!, London. 78: Courtesy Victoria and Albert Museum (museum no. IS39 1950), London. 79: Courtesy Victoria and Albert Museum (museum no. IS2542), London. 80, 81: Courtesy 1st The Queen's Dragoon Guards, Carver Barracks, Saffron Walden, Essex, England. 82-85: Associated Press Ltd., London. 86, 87: Steve McCurry, New York. 89: Nehru Memorial Museum, New Delhi. 91: David Beatty, Bath, England — artwork by Chapman Bounford, London. 92, 93: Cary Sawhney, Brookman's Park, Hertfordshire, England. 94: Michael Freeman, London. 96: Digitized image by Ralph Scott/Chapman Bounford, London. 97: Pablo Bartholomew, Bombay. 98, 99: Raghubir Singh from The John Hillelson Agency, London. 101: Penny Tweedie from Daily Telegraph Color Library, London. 102: Dilip Mehta from Colorific!, London. 103: Adam Woolfitt from Susan Griggs Agency, London. 104-109: Pablo Bartholomew, Bombay. 110: Steve McCurry, New York. 113: Raghu Rai from The John Hillelson Agency, London. 114, 115: Steve McCurry, New York — Pablo Bartholomew, Bombay; Sybil Sassoon from Robert Harding Picture Library, London. 116: Jana Koldrt, Zurich. 117: Ann and Bury Peerless, Birchington-on-Sea, Kent, England. 118: Michael Freeman, London. 119-121: Raghubir Singh from The John Hillelson Agency, London. 122: Michael Freeman, London. 123: Raghubir Singh from The John Hillelson Agency, London. 124, 125: Sybil Sassoon from Robert Harding Picture Library, London. 126-137: Pablo Bartholomew, Bombay. 138-141: George Shelley, New York. 142: Homer Sykes from Impact Photos, London. 143: Raghubir Singh from The John Hillelson Agency, London. 144: Michael Freeman, London. 145: Tom Owen Edmunds, London. 146, 147: Raghubir Singh from The John Hillelson Agency, London. 148: Steve McCurry, New York. 149: Pierre Toutain, Paris. 150-152: Christopher Cormack from Impact Photos, London. 153: Pablo Bartholomew, Bombay. 155: Michael Freeman, London.

BIBLIOGRAPHY

BOOKS

Akbar, M. J., *India: The Siege Within.* Middlesex, England: Penguin Books, 1985.

Allen, Charles, ed., *Plain Tales from the Raj.* London: André Deutsch, 1975.

Allen, Charles, and Sharada Dwivedi, *Lives of the Indian Princes.* London: Century Publishing Company, 1984.

Baroda, the Maharaja of, *The Palaces of India.* London: William Collins Sons and Company, 1980.

Cambridge Economic History of India. 2 vols. Cambridge, England: Cambridge University Press, 1982.

Carstairs, G. M.:

Death of a Witch. London: Hutchinson, 1983.

The Twice-Born. London: The Hogarth Press, 1957.

Cassen, R. H., *India: Population, Economy, Society.* London: The Macmillan Press, 1978.

Chaudhuri, Nirad C.:

Autobiography of an Unknown Indian. London: Macmillan and Company, 1951.

Hinduism. London: Chatto and Windus, 1979.

Collins, Larry, and Dominique Lapierre, *Freedom at Midnight.* London: Pan Books, 1977.

Dumont, Louis, *Homo Hierarchicus.* London: Paladin Books, 1972.

Durrans, Brian, and Robert Knox, *India, Past into Present.* London: British Museum Publications, 1982.

Dyson, K. K., *A Various Universe.* Delhi: Oxford University Press, 1978.

Eck, Diana L., *Banaras: City of Light.* London: Routledge and Kegan Paul, 1983.

Edwardes, Michael, *Indian Temples and Palaces.* London: Paul Hamlyn, 1969.

Farmer, B. H., *An Introduction to South Asia.* London: Methuen and Company, 1983.

Fishlock, Trevor, *India File.* London: John Murray, 1983.

Fürer-Haimendorf, Christoph von, *Tribes of India.* Berkeley, California: University of California Press, 1982.

Gray, Basil, ed., *The Arts of India.* Oxford, England: Phaidon, 1981.

Hiro, Dilip:

Inside India Today. London: Routledge and Kegan Paul, 1976.

The Untouchables of India. London: Minority Rights Group, 1984.

Hobson, Sarah, *Family Web: A Story of India.* London: John Murray, 1978.

Hutton, J. H., *Caste in India.* Cambridge, England: Cambridge University Press, 1946.

India: A Reference Annual. Ministry of Information and Broadcasting, Government of India. Published annually.

India: A Travel Survival Kit. Emeryville, California: Lonely Planet Publications, 1984.

Ions, Veronica, *Indian Mythology.* London: Paul Hamlyn, 1967.

Johnson, B.L.C., *India: Resources and Development.* London: Heinemann Educational Books, 1979.

Kaul, H. K., ed., *Travellers' India: An Anthology.* New Delhi: Oxford University Press, 1979.

Keay, John, *India Discovered: The Achievement of the British Raj.* Leicester, England: Windward, 1981.

Kishwar, Madhu, and Ruth Vanita, *In Search of Answers: Indian Women's Voices from Manushi.* London: Zed Books, 1984.

Kolenda, Pauline, *Caste in Contemporary India: Beyond Organic Solidarity.* Menlo Park, California: Benjamin-Cummings Publishing Company, 1978.

Lannoy, Richard, *The Speaking Tree.* London: Oxford University Press, 1971.

Mehta, Ved:

A Family Affair: India under Three Prime Ministers. Oxford, England: Oxford University Press, 1982.

Portrait of India. London: Weidenfeld and Nicolson, 1970.

Michell, George, *The Hindu Temple.* London: Paul Elek, 1977.

Mohanti, Prafulla, *My Village, My Life.* London: Davis-Poynter, 1973.

Moorhouse, Geoffrey:

Calcutta. Middlesex, England: Penguin Books, 1983.

India Britannica. London: Harvill Press, 1983.

Moraes, Dom, *Bombay* (The Great Cities series). Amsterdam: Time-Life International, 1979.

Naipaul, V. S., *An Area of Darkness.* London: André Deutsch, 1964.

Nehru, Jawaharlal, *The Discovery of India.* London: Meridian Books, 1946.

Nyrop, Richard F., et al., *Area Handbook for India* (Foreign Area Studies series, American University). Washington, D.C.: U.S. Government Printing Office, 1975.

Rushbrook Williams, L. F., *A Handbook for Travellers in India, Pakistan, Nepal, Bangladesh and Sri Lanka.* London: John Murray, 1975.

Segal, Ronald, *The Crisis of India.* London: Jonathan Cape, 1965.

Shackle, Christopher, *The Sikhs.* London: Minority Rights Group, 1984.

Spate, O.H.K., and A.T.A. Learmonth, *India and Pakistan: A General and Regional Geography.* London: Methuen and Company, 1967.

Spear, Percival, *A History of India.* Vol. 2. Middlesex, England: Penguin Books, 1965.

Thapar, Romila, *A History of India.* Vol. 1. Middlesex, England: Penguin Books, 1966.

Tindall, Gillian, *City of Gold: The Biography of Bombay.* London: Temple Smith, 1982.

Walker, Benjamin, *Hindu World: An Encyclopedic Survey of Hinduism.* 2 vols. London: George Allen and Unwin, 1968.

Watson, Francis, *A Concise History of India.* London: Thames and Hudson, 1979.

Wheeler, Sir Mortimer, *The Indus Civilization.* Cambridge, England: Cambridge University Press, 1968.

Wolpert, Stanley, *A New History of India.* Oxford, England: Oxford University Press, 1982.

World Development Report, 1984. Oxford, England: Oxford University Press, 1984.

PERIODICALS

"By Rail across India," *National Geographic,* June 1984.

"India," *Financial Times* survey, June 11, 1984.

"India: The Major Industries," *Guardian* special report, March 22 and 23, 1982.

"Monsoons," *National Geographic,* December 1984.

"Mrs. Gandhi: A Woman of Action, Political Instinct, but Little Vision," *Guardian,* November 1, 1984.

"Mrs. Indira Gandhi," the London *Times,* November 1, 1984.

"New Delhi: India's Mirror," *National Geographic,* April 1985.

"The Sikhs: Ferocity and Faith," *Geo,* February 1984.

"When the Moguls Ruled," *National Geographic,* April 1985.

INDEX

Numerals in italics indicate an illustration of the subject mentioned.

H

I

J

K

L

M

N

O

P

Q

R

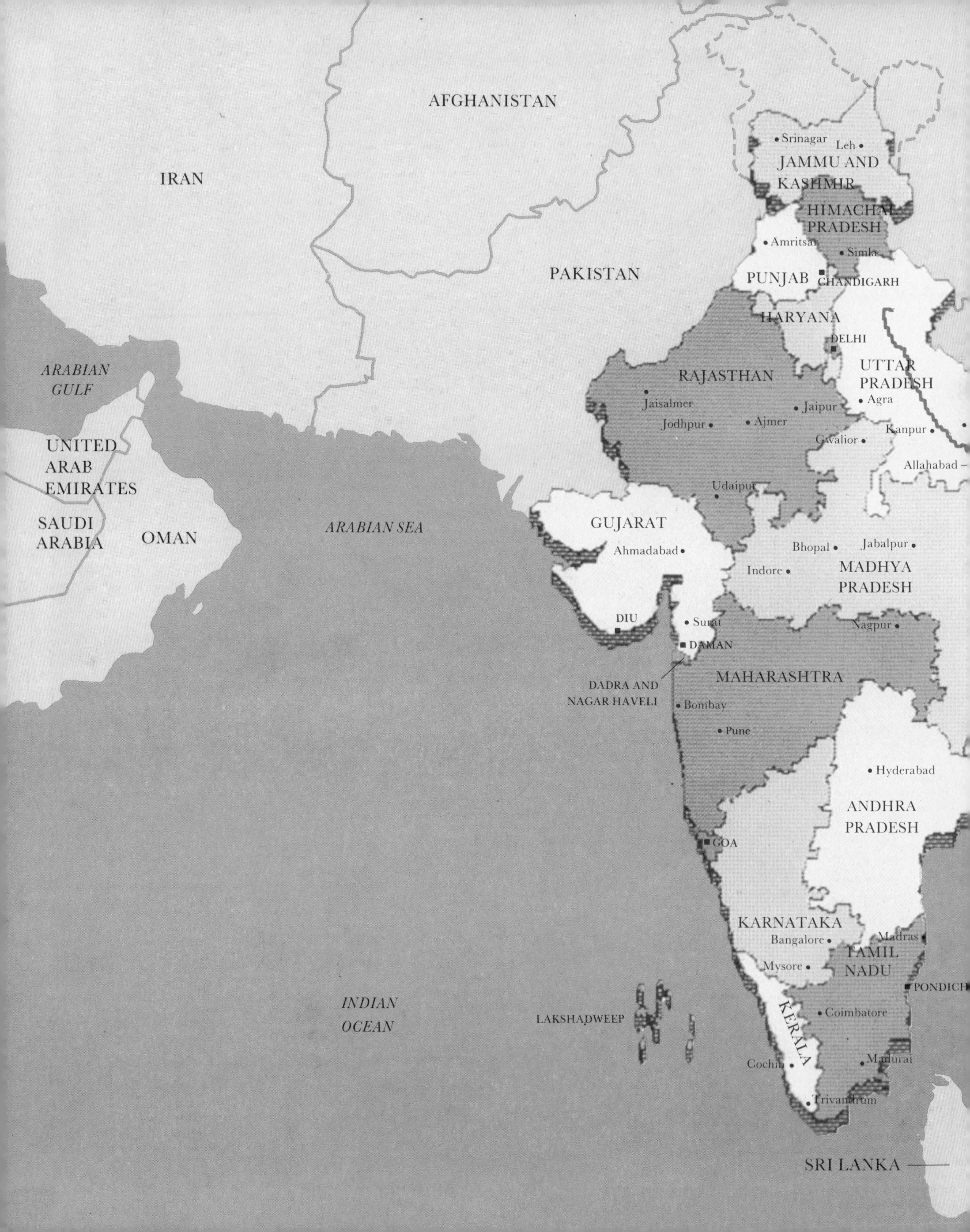
AFGHANISTAN
IRAN
PAKISTAN
ARABIAN GULF
UNITED ARAB EMIRATES
SAUDI ARABIA
OMAN
ARABIAN SEA
INDIAN OCEAN
LAKSHADWEEP
SRI LANKA
Srinagar
Leh
JAMMU AND KASHMIR
HIMACHAL PRADESH
Amritsar
Simla
PUNJAB
CHANDIGARH
HARYANA
DELHI
RAJASTHAN
UTTAR PRADESH
Jaisalmer
Jodhpur
Ajmer
Jaipur
Agra
Kanpur
Gwalior
Allahabad
Udaipur
GUJARAT
Ahmadabad
Bhopal
Jabalpur
Indore
MADHYA PRADESH
DIU
Surat
DAMAN
Nagpur
DADRA AND NAGAR HAVELI
MAHARASHTRA
Bombay
Pune
Hyderabad
ANDHRA PRADESH
GOA
KARNATAKA
Bangalore
Madras
Mysore
TAMIL NADU
PONDICH
Coimbatore
KERALA
Cochin
Madurai
Trivandrum